# 103 Questions Children Ask about RIGHT FROM WRONG®

## Written by:

David R. Veerman, M.Div.
James C. Galvin, Ed.D.
James C. Wilhoit, Ph.D.
Daryl J. Lucas
Richard Osborne
Lil Crump

Tyndale House Publishers, Inc. Wheaton, Illinois

**Library of Congress Cataloging-in-Publication Data**

103 questions children ask about right from wrong / David R. Veerman
. . . [et al.].
    p.    cm.
  ISBN 0-8423-4595-7 (SC);  ISBN 0-8423-4599-X (SPECIAL EDITION)
  1. Christian education of children.  2. Christian ethics—Study
and teaching.  3. Children—Conduct of life.  4. Children—Religious
life.  5. Christian education—Home training.  I. Veerman, David.
BV1475.2.A18  1995
241'.07—dc20                             95-24130

Printed in the United States of America

01  00  99  98  97  96  95
11  10  9  8  7  6  5  4  3  2  1

# CONTENTS

# INTRODUCTION *by Josh McDowell*

When my daughter, Kelly, was in fourth grade, several students in her class swiped an object off the teacher's desk while the teacher was out of the room. The children only wanted to play with the object, but it soon broke, and they returned it to its previous place on the teacher's desk.

When the teacher discovered the damage, she asked one of Kelly's classmates what had happened. The girl yielded to the pressure of the group and lied. Then the teacher asked Kelly. Kelly explained matter-of-factly what had happened.

The next day I took Kelly out for breakfast and told her she'd done the right thing, in spite of any pressure or harassment she may get from her classmates.

"Honey," I then asked, "why is lying wrong?"

"Because the Bible says it's wrong," she answered.

"Why does the Bible say it's wrong?"

"Because God commanded it."

"Why did God command it?"

"I don't know," she admitted.

I took her hands in mine and locked eyes with her. "Because God is truth, Kelly. Truth comes from his nature, and whatever is contrary to God's nature is sin."

It was not enough for Kelly simply to know that lying was wrong or even that the Bible states that it's wrong. If we are going to keep the culture from capturing our kids and instill biblical values in them, they must know *why* certain things are right and *why* certain things are wrong.

Let me explain.

You and I live in challenging times. Our newspapers report it: "Drugs Sold by Children," "Violence Erupts in Classroom," "Crime Takes over Streets." News magazines document it: "The fraying of America's moral fabric has become a national obsession; 76 percent of Americans think we're in a spiritual and moral decline, according to a recent *Newsweek* poll." The Christian community fears it: "Based on a recent survey, the number one fear among Christian parents (pastors and youth leaders) is they will not be able to pass on their values to the next generation."

That is why we are collaborating with over forty denominational and parachurch leaders **"to launch a nationwide grassroots effort to resource parents, grandparents, pastors, youth workers, children's workers, and Christian educators to equip youth and children to know right from wrong, enabling them to make right choices."**

## Kids are confused about truth

Many of our youth are struggling with the concept of what truth is and who defines it. Our study indicates that our kids are confused about which truths are absolute and what makes them absolute. And if this is true of our teenagers, you can be certain our younger children are just as confused. Consequently, they are making conditional decisions, choosing what seems to be in their best interests at the time, without reference to any underlying principles to guide their behavior.

## What is absolute truth?

Many of our kids simply do not understand or accept absolute truth—that is, that which is **true for all people, for all times, for all places.** Absolute truth is truth that is objective, universal, and constant.

We all have established various family rules and guidelines. For example, I have established a curfew with my thirteen-year-old daughter, specifying what time she should be home after a football game. I have told her, "It is not good to stay out later than 11:00." I have set a firm guideline to be followed. If she obeys the curfew, she is right; if she violates it, she is wrong. I want my daughter to consider it a hard-and-fast rule. And, in most cases, she does.

But should we consider that guideline—to be home by 11:00 after every football game—an *absolute* truth? No. It is not applicable to all people, at all times, in all places. Parents, communities, states, and governments may create various ordinances, regulations, and laws that are to be obeyed, but they are not necessarily absolutes. Ordinances change, regulations expire, and some laws only apply in certain states. In fact, even the curfew rules for my daughter may change someday. An absolute truth, on the other hand, is objective, universal, and constant.

If our children are going to learn how to discern right from wrong, they must know what truths are absolute and why. They need to know what standards of behavior are right for all people, for all times, for all places. They need to know who determines truth—and why.

### Why truth matters

You may say, "Come on, Josh, all this talk about absolutes seems so abstract. Do you really think my children's views about truth will make a difference in their behavior?" That is one of the astounding insights of our research. The study indicates that when our kids do not accept an objective standard of truth they become:

> 36 percent more likely to lie to you as a parent!
> 48 percent more likely to cheat on an exam!
> 2 times more likely to try to physically hurt someone!
> 2 times more likely to watch a pornographic film!
> 2 times more likely to steal!
> 3 times more likely to use illegal drugs!
> 6 times more likely to attempt suicide!

If your children fail to embrace truth as an objective standard that governs their lives, the study shows it will make them:

65 percent more likely to mistrust people!
2 times more likely to be disappointed!
2 times more likely to be angry with life!
2 times more likely to be resentful!

How our kids think about truth has a definite effect on their behavior—the choices they make and the attitudes they adopt.

## There is hope

It's a frightening prospect to raise our children "around tough and crooked people" (Philippians 2:15). There are no easy answers, but there is hope. It is not too late to reinforce the crumbling foundations. If you and I are willing to set aside the quick-fix mentality and face the stark reality of what we as a Christian community have allowed (and perhaps unwittingly adopted ourselves), I believe there is hope.

## What are the Four Cs?

The Four Cs is a four-step approach to making right choices. The hope is that it will create a new way of thinking and acting as a child learns how to make right choices based on God and his Word as the standard of right and wrong. Here's the process:

1. *Consider the choice.* We want our children, when faced with a moral choice, to first stop and consider what determines its rightness or wrongness.

The culture has conditioned many to believe that individuals have the right to determine for themselves what is right and wrong. Truth, in this view, is subjective and personal; there is no absolute right or wrong that governs a person's life. In other words, it's up to the individual to determine the rightness and wrongness of his or her own attitudes or actions.

In this first step we must ask: "Who determines what is right or wrong in this situation?" This step erects a stop sign of sorts to alert our children that their attitudes and actions are judged by someone other than themselves, and they are not to justify their behavior based on their own selfish interests.

2. *Compare it to God.* This next step answers the question: Who determines what is right and wrong absolutely? Here we want our children to acknowledge the fact that there is an absolute, righteous God and that they must compare their attitudes and actions to him and his Word to determine whether they are right or wrong.

This step points them to the revelation of Jehovah God in his written Word. His Word, the Bible, gives all of us specific and absolute guidelines as to the rightness or wrongness of attitudes and actions. And these guidelines are not simply the do's and don'ts of the law—they are a reflection of the very nature and character of God himself.

3. *Commit to God's way.* This third step is where the rubber meets the road—this is decision time. Considering the choice and comparing it to God are necessary steps to show our children that their ways are not like God's ways. It shows all of us that our tendency is to justify, rationalize, and excuse ourselves, all in an attempt to legitimize our selfish interests and pleasures. When we compare our attitudes and actions to God as God (step 2), we *admit* that his character and nature define right and wrong absolutely. Those attitudes and actions that are like him are considered right, and those attitudes and actions that are not like him are considered wrong.

Then when we commit to God's way, it means we turn from our selfishness and those attitudes and actions in question that are unlike him. We *submit* to him as Lord of our lives and rely on his power to live out his way in us.

*4. Count on God's protection and provision.* When we humbly *admit* God's sovereignty and sincerely *submit* to his loving authority, we can not only begin to see clearly the distinctions between right and wrong, but we can also count on God's protection and provision. Here in this fourth step we want our children to thank God for his loving protection and provision. This doesn't mean everything will be rosy; in fact, God says that we may suffer for righteousness' sake. But such suffering has great rewards. Living according to God's way and allowing the Holy Spirit to live through us bring many spiritual blessings, like freedom from guilt, a clear conscience, the joy of sharing Christ, and—most important—the love and smile of God in our lives. Additionally, we enjoy many physical, emotional, psychological, and relational benefits when we are obedient to God. While God's protection and provision should not be our children's primary motivation to obey him, it provides a powerful reinforcement for them to choose the right and reject the wrong.

Children need to know that God truly cares about the choices they make. "'For I know the plans I have for you,' says the Lord. 'They are plans for good and not for evil. I want to give you a future and a hope'" (Jeremiah 29:11). Ultimately, making right moral choices based upon God and his Word as our standard of right and wrong comes down to trusting God. Do we really believe God has a plan for our good? If he does—and I assure you he does—then living in relationship with him is not only right, it is in our long-term best interest.

This book will enable you to lead children to discover that a personal relationship with God is not only possible but is critical to their making right moral choices in life.

You play a vital role in helping them understand that relationship. Together, with God's help, we can help children learn how to make right moral choices and help them discover a new and fresh relationship with God as well.

—Josh

P.S. To help you and your church's ongoing effort to pass on biblical values to the next generation, we have provided a listing of additional resources at the end of this book.

# NOTE FROM THE WRITERS

This book is a launching pad. It's not an exhaustive list of all the questions your child will ever have about morality. It's not a compilation of all the answers you'll ever need. It's a collection of the Big Ones—questions that you're very likely to hear children ask if you're around them for very long—and a road map to some answers.

The questions come entirely from real children. We surveyed children ages three to twelve and collected their responses, then sorted them (the questions, not the children) until we identified the 103 most common and important ones. If you are a parent or if you work with children very often, you will surely hear questions like these sooner or later—if you haven't already!

The answers, however, come entirely from Scripture. For every question, we looked in the Bible for the most relevant passages, then summarized their application to the issues the question raised. Study the Scriptures listed with each question, because the Bible is our final authority. God's Word alone reveals God's will to us, and God's will comes entirely from his perfect, holy nature.

We wrote this book to help you answer kids' questions about right and wrong. We sincerely hope and pray it does that.

But sooner or later your child will need to learn how to make those choices when no one is around to help. To that end, we have provided an explanation of the Four Cs, by Josh McDowell, in the introduction. This four-step approach to decision making is a skill every child should have. Learn it and teach it to your child as you discuss the questions and answers he or she has.

May God bless you as you strive to help your child choose right from wrong.

—Dave Veerman, Jim Galvin, Jim Wilhoit,
Daryl Lucas, Rick Osborne, Lil Crump

# RIGHT
### AND
# WRONG,
# RIGHT?

## 1

**A:** We can know what is right by knowing God. God is perfect and always right, so everything good matches what God is like. For example, we know it is right to be loving and kind because God is love. Everything that is wrong goes against what God is like. We can learn what God is like by reading his Word, the Bible. The Bible helps us know how to be like God and act as he does. God has given us rules and guidance for how to live. Those are also in the Bible. When we read rules such as the Ten Commandments, we know how God wants us to act.

---

**KEY VERSE:** *Be careful to obey all of these commands. You must do what is right in the eyes of the Lord your God. If you do, all will go well with you and your children forever. (Deuteronomy 12:28)*

**RELATED VERSES:** *Exodus 20:1-17; Deuteronomy 5:6-22; John 14:6; 2 Timothy 3:16-17*

**RELATED QUESTIONS:** *How can everyone know what is right and what is wrong? My friends do things that I think are wrong—how do I know if they are right or not? Could it ever be wrong to do something I think is right? Why is New Age wrong?*

**NOTE TO PARENTS:** *A child may use this question as an excuse to disobey you or to be disrespectful to teachers and others in authority. "How do you know that such and such is wrong?" God determines what is right and wrong, but he also tells children to honor and obey their parents and to respect the authorities. Encourage your children to trust God and his Word, because he wants the best for us.*

# Q: WHY DO PEOPLE DO WRONG WHEN THEY KNOW THAT IT'S WRONG?

## 2

**A:** People do wrong because of their sinful nature. Many, many years ago, God created the first man and woman, Adam and Eve. But soon afterward, Adam and Eve committed the first sin—they disobeyed God. You can read about it in Genesis 3:1-24. Before then, the world was perfect, with no sin, evil, or wrongdoing. But when Adam and Eve disobeyed God, sin entered the world, and ever since then everyone has been born with a sinful nature. In other words, people find it *natural* to do what is wrong; they find it easy to choose to do wrong. This is a weakness that all people have. Sometimes people will do something even when they know it is wrong because they are afraid of what others will say if they do right. They might feel pressured by friends to do wrong. They might have a bad habit. It's not that everything they do is wrong; they can do good and make right choices, too. But they find it easy to make the wrong choices. People still have the same choice today that Adam and Eve had. We can trust God and follow his way, or we can decide for ourselves what is right and wrong and do it our own way, the wrong way.

---

**KEY VERSE:** *When Adam sinned, sin entered the whole human race. His sin spread death through all the world. Everything began to grow old and die because all sinned. (Romans 5:12)*

**RELATED VERSES:** *Genesis 3:1-24; Isaiah 53:6; Matthew 26:41; Mark 14:38; Romans 6:23*

**NOTE TO PARENTS:** *Give hope that your child can do right; the fact that there is sin doesn't mean a person has to do wrong. This may be the time to explain that Jesus came to die for us and that through faith in him we can be free from the power of sin in our lives.*

# Q: WHY IS IT WRONG TO BE BAD?

## 3

**A:** It is wrong to be bad because God created us to do good. Think about your bicycle. It was made for riding, for helping you go from one place to another faster and easier than walking. If you tried to use your bike to scrape snow off the sidewalk or to ride across a lake, it wouldn't work—and it would mess up your bike, too. That's not what your bike was made for. In the same way, God designed us to do what is good and right, to bring honor to him. When we do bad things, we do what we were not created to do. God created everything; he knows what works and what doesn't, and he knows what will make us happy and what will hurt us. And he loves us! If we trust him, we will do things his way.

---

**KEY VERSE:** *It is God himself who has made us what we are. He has given us new lives from Christ Jesus. Long ago he planned that we should spend our lives in helping others. (Ephesians 2:10)*

**RELATED VERSES:** *Romans 3:23; Ephesians 1:5-6*

**RELATED QUESTIONS:** *Why is it wrong to do bad things? Why can I do certain things and not others? Why is it bad to do certain things and not others? Why should I be good?*

**NOTE TO PARENTS:** *It may be helpful to save the word* wrong *for moral issues. You could avoid saying, for example, that it's wrong to wear stripes with polka dots. Unusual habits or choice of clothing may invite criticism from peers, but it's not wrong in the sense of being morally wrong. This makes a clear distinction between wrongdoing and bad taste.*

# Q: HOW DID GOD DECIDE WHAT WAS WRONG AND WHAT WAS RIGHT?

## 4

**A:** God didn't have a meeting with the angels and announce that some actions were right and some actions were wrong. He is perfect and right. God's very nature is good, and whatever he does is right. And anything that is against God's nature is wrong. God's rules in the Bible tell us what God is like.

Remember also that God tells us what is right and wrong because he loves us. His rules protect us and guide us. It's like our telling a baby not to touch a hot stove. We want to keep the baby from getting hurt. We make the rule because we love the baby. God tells us what to do for the same reason. He wants to take care of us, to make us joyful, and to help us live.

**KEY VERSE:** *You are to be perfect, even as your Father in Heaven is perfect. (Matthew 5:48)*

**RELATED VERSES:** *Psalm 118:29; Jeremiah 33:11; Micah 6:8; Nahum 1:7; John 14:6; 1 Peter 1:15-16*

**RELATED QUESTIONS:** *How do I know if a person is good or bad? Why are right and wrong different?*

**NOTE TO PARENTS:** *You can often explain the usefulness of rules by drawing examples from the rules that adults "force" on very young children. For example, we don't let babies play in the toilet, break things, or toddle into the street, because we love them and want to protect them. Even more important, babies don't understand these rules. They just have to obey them. Even a four- or five-year-old can understand that all of God's rules, in a similar way, come out of his love and care for us—even if we don't always understand how.*

# Q: ARE THINGS ALWAYS EITHER RIGHT OR WRONG?

## 5

**A:** Not every choice we make is either *right* or *wrong*. Sometimes we just like certain things more than others—such as ice cream flavors. If you like strawberry, it isn't right or wrong—it's just something you like. Or you might have two toys to play with, and you choose one over the other. Both would be all right, but you chose one. At other times, we have to choose between what is *good,* what is *better,* and what is *best*. None of those choices would be bad or wrong, but we would be wise to choose what is best. In choices like those, parents and other wise people can give us good advice. Some choices are either right or wrong, but not *all* choices are.

---

**KEY VERSES:** *You are free to eat food offered to idols if you want to. It's not against God's laws to eat such meat. But that doesn't mean that you should go ahead and do it. It may be legal, but it may not be best and helpful. Don't think only of yourself. Try to do what is best for others. (1 Corinthians 10:23-24)*

**RELATED VERSES:** *Galatians 5:1, 13-26; James 1:5*

**NOTE TO PARENTS:** *Again, be careful about how you use the word* wrong. *An absolute moral wrong, such as stealing, doesn't have the same "wrongness" as a matter of etiquette, such as what to say to a hostess about the food. Absolute right or wrong is that which is right or wrong for all people, at all times, in all places.*

## 6

**A:** Living in a "free country" means that our highest laws guarantee our right to say and do certain things, not that our country doesn't cost us anything. For example, we have freedom of speech, freedom of the press, and freedom of religion. That means we can say, publish, and worship pretty much whatever we want. But we don't have total freedom, because our country needs laws and rules so that everything will run smoothly. That is, the freedom we do have works because we have limits on it. Governments need money for paying leaders, police officers, firefighters, teachers, and other workers, and for building and repairing things like bridges and roads. The citizens provide this money by paying taxes and tolls. The laws of a country are not the same as God's laws, but God tells us to respect the government and to obey its laws. So we pay tolls, wear seat belts, stop at red traffic lights, and follow the speed limits.

---

**KEY VERSE:** *For the Lord's sake, obey every law of your government. Obey the laws of the king as head of the state. (1 Peter 2:13)*

**RELATED VERSES:** *Romans 13:1-3; Colossians 2:10; 1 Timothy 2:1-2; 1 Peter 2:13-17*

**RELATED QUESTIONS:** *Why do I have to wear my seat belt? Why do kids ride their bikes when cars are coming?*

**NOTE TO PARENTS:** *You can explain to your child that God wants us to obey the government because he established it. The rules that the government makes are meant to keep us safe.*

# Q: IF THE LAW SAYS SOMETHING IS RIGHT BUT GOD SAYS IT'S WRONG, WHO'S RIGHT?

## 7

**A:** The Bible tells us to obey the government. But when a government law goes against what God wants us to do, we should obey God instead of the government. God is in charge of the government and not the other way around. For example, if the government passed a law making it illegal to pray, we should break the law and pray anyway. The same would be true about worshiping God, reading the Bible, and telling others about Christ. And if the government were to make it OK to lie and steal, we still shouldn't do those things because they go against God's law. God created and rules the universe. No one can have higher authority than God. So we must always obey him first.

**KEY VERSE:** *Peter and the apostles replied, "We must obey God rather than men." (Acts 5:29)*

**RELATED VERSES:** *Daniel 3:5-23; 6:1-28; Romans 13:1-3; 1 Peter 2:13-17*

**RELATED QUESTIONS:** *Why do governments make such stupid rules? How come adults can swear and smoke but I can't?*

**NOTE TO PARENTS:** *This could be a good opportunity to explain to your child that God is the ultimate authority on what is right. His standards are right for all people, all times, all places—whether the government agrees or not.*

## 8

**A:** Morals are standards for right and wrong living. Morals are rules that we follow for doing one thing and not another. Different people live by many different sets of morals—what they think is best or fair or right. But only what God says about these things is right for all people everywhere all the time. God has only one set of morals that he wants everyone to follow. A person who lives by God's morals doesn't steal because that's God's standard, not just because the person doesn't like to steal.

---

**KEY VERSE:** *Don't you know that those doing such things can't share in God's Kingdom? Don't fool yourselves. If you live in sin, worship idols, are an adulterer or homosexual you can't share his Kingdom. (1 Corinthians 6:9)*

**RELATED VERSES:** *Ephesians 5:1, 5; James 1:21*

**RELATED QUESTIONS:** *What does ethics mean? Is ethics like ethnic food? Are morals those animals that dig in the ground and make holes in your garden?*

**NOTE TO PARENTS:** *It may be difficult to explain the difference between a nice person and a moral person. A nice person is concerned about what other people think and doesn't want to hurt other people's feelings. A moral person is conerned about what God thinks and wants to follow God's rules for thinking, talking, and doing what is right all the time.*

# Q: HOW CAN I TELL RIGHT FROM WRONG?

## 9

**A:** Anything that goes against what God is like is wrong. We can discover what God is like by reading his Word, the Bible. The Bible also tells us what God wants us to do. So we can tell right from wrong by asking: Will this disobey a law that God has given us? (For example, "no stealing," "no lying," "love your neighbor," or "honor your father and mother.") Anything that breaks one of God's laws is wrong.

If we are faced with a choice that God hasn't given us a law about (or if we don't know where to find it in the Bible), we can ask: Will doing this go against my conscience? We can also ask: Will it hurt someone? If the answer is yes to either question, then most likely we should not do it.

Another question to ask is: Why am I doing this? If it's only because of pressure from friends or because of fear, then it may not be right. This is when we must carefully consider the choice that we have to make. We must think about what we know about God, pray for wisdom, and make the *best* choice we can.

---

**KEY VERSE:** *A good man produces good deeds from a good heart. And an evil man produces evil deeds from his hidden wickedness. Whatever is in the heart overflows into speech. (Luke 6:45)*

**NOTE TO PARENTS:** *We need to cultivate character in our children and not just give them rules for behavior, because most of our moral acts come from our tendencies and habits. So we should teach our children the principles behind the precepts and ultimately point them to the person who embodies them, God himself. That is how our children will learn to tell right from wrong.*

# GOD,
## THE
# BIBLE,
## AND
# CONSCIENCE

## 10

**A:** God has given us his Word, the Bible, which tells us about him and how he wants us to live. So we must do our best to obey what God tells us in his Word. Jesus said that the most important rule (called a commandment) is "'Love the Lord your God with all your heart, soul, and mind.' This is the first and greatest command. The second most important is similar: 'Love your neighbor as much as you love yourself'" (Matthew 22:37-39). We should love God first and then other people. If we do that, we will do what is right.

Also, God wants us to develop a desire for the best, not just second-best. Some activities may not be wrong but aren't best for us. We should do what is *best* and not settle for anything less. Making right, moral choices means not just saying no to bad actions but also saying yes to what is good and helpful.

---

**KEY VERSES:** *Jesus said, "'Love the Lord your God with all your heart, soul, and mind.' This is the first and greatest command. The second most important is similar: 'Love your neighbor as much as you love yourself.'" (Matthew 22:37-39)*

**RELATED VERSES:** *Exodus 20:1-17; Deuteronomy 5:6-22*

**NOTE TO PARENTS:** *A child may think that being good means just avoiding the bad. Help your child to see that being good means making a positive choice to please God in everything we do. And we seek to do so because we know that God seeks our best.*

# Q:
## WHEN I ASK A QUESTION, WHY DO YOU ALWAYS TELL ME WHAT THE BIBLE SAYS?

## 11

**A:** The Bible is God's Word. When we read it, we learn what God is like and how he wants us to live in this world. Think of the Bible as an instruction book, like the one for the family car. If we do what the book says, the car will run right. If something goes wrong, we can read the book and find out how to fix it. The Bible is God's instruction book for our lives. We need to read and study it so that we will run right and so God can fix things that go wrong with us. It's not enough just to read the Bible; we also must do what it says.

---

**KEY VERSE:** *The whole Bible was given to us by inspiration from God. It is useful to teach us what is true. It helps us to know what is wrong in our lives. It straightens us out and helps us do what is right. (2 Timothy 3:16)*

**RELATED VERSE:** *Psalm 119:105*

**RELATED QUESTION:** *Why do you have to read the Bible so much?*

**NOTE TO PARENTS:** *One of the most powerful ways to help your child learn right from wrong is to read a Bible verse together that deals with a specific moral issue (such as honesty or lying) and then talk about how this might affect your own family life. For example, you could read Ephesians 4:25 and then call to mind the last time your child spoke the truth when it was difficult to do so. Perhaps you asked your child, "What are you doing?" and your child spoke honestly, despite being afraid of getting into trouble. This will reinforce the moral principle as well as its importance.*

# Q: IS IT A SIN IF YOU'RE NOT SURE IF SOMETHING IS WRONG BUT YOU STILL GO ALONG WITH IT?

## 12

# A:

It is not necessarily a sin to do something that we don't know is right or wrong. We can't know everything, and we shouldn't assume that everything we don't know about is wrong. On the other hand, if you have doubts and think it *might* be wrong, you'd better make sure before doing it. Put off doing it; then read the Bible and ask Mom or Dad. Remember, you should choose what is best, not just avoid what is wrong.

---

**KEY VERSE:** *Anyone who believes that something he wants to do is wrong shouldn't do it. He sins if he does. He thinks it is wrong, and so for him it is wrong. Anything that is done apart from what he feels is right is sin. (Romans 14:23)*

**RELATED VERSE:** *1 Corinthians 4:4*

**RELATED QUESTION:** *If you know you are doing something bad and your parents said you're allowed to do it, is it right or wrong?*

**NOTE TO PARENTS:** *This touches on the issue of peer pressure. Kids don't always know what is right and wrong. They really don't. Whenever your kids report that they avoided doing something that they weren't quite sure about, affirm them. This may also be a good time to explain the Four Cs: Consider the choice, Compare our attitudes and actions to God, Commit to God's ways, and Count on God's protection and provision.*

# Q: WHAT IS A CONSCIENCE?

## 13

**A:** God has built into us a way of helping us tell right from wrong. We call this inner voice our *conscience,* and we need to learn to listen to it. It's a feeling inside about something we are thinking about doing. If what we are thinking about doing is not right, then our conscience can make us feel bad about it and give us the sense that we should not do it. Our conscience can also tell us when we *should* do something. When it does that, we get a strong sense that we should do what we're thinking about. God gave us our conscience to help us decide what to do. So it's important for us to listen to our conscience.

If we don't listen to our conscience, pretty soon we get into the habit of ignoring it. After a while we won't hear it at all. That can lead to trouble. Listen carefully to your conscience.

---

**KEY VERSE:** *Because of this, I try to keep my conscience clean before God and man. (Acts 24:16)*

**RELATED VERSES:** *1 Peter 3:16; Romans 2:15; 1 Corinthians 4:4*

**RELATED QUESTION:** *Once I know what's right, do I have to do it?*

**NOTE TO PARENTS:** *Be careful not to associate the conscience only with guilty feelings. The best decisions for what is right and good come out of a firm conviction and desire to do right, not out of a desire to silence a guilty conscience. When discussing the conscience with kids, emphasize the positive role it can have. The more we read and study God's Word, the more our conscience can help us choose to do right.*

# Q: DO I HAVE TO LET LITTLE KIDS IN MY ROOM TO PLAY WHEN I HAVE SPECIAL STUFF?

## 14

**A:** Maybe. God is loving and kind, so he wants us to be loving and kind, too, not stingy and selfish. If friends, brothers or sisters, or small children want to play with your toys, you should let them if it's safe and OK with their parents. Sometimes we act as if our toys, clothes, and other belongings are more important than our friends and family. But it's good to take turns and to let other people enjoy our "special stuff." When we do that, people will be able to see that we are different from people who don't love Jesus.

On the other hand, God wants us to be responsible, too. Although God is loving and kind, he would not give us something that would hurt us. You don't have to let little kids do whatever they want with your things, especially if your special stuff is fragile or too hard for little kids to use right. Everybody should take good care of their things, and everyone should respect everyone else's things. Try to let other kids have a turn with your stuff whenever you can, and when you can't, be kind about it and make sure you have a good reason.

---

**KEY VERSE:** *Love is very patient and kind. It is never jealous or envious. It never boasts or is proud. (1 Corinthians 13:4)*

**RELATED VERSES:** *Galatians 5:22; James 4:17*

**RELATED QUESTION:** *Is it right to stand up for your rights?*

**NOTE TO PARENTS:** *This touches on the issue of sharing. Place the emphasis on taking turns rather than on sharing; children will more easily understand what you're asking them to do.*

# Q: HOW DO I BECOME EVEN CLOSER TO GOD THAN I AM NOW?

## 15

**A:** Think of God as someone who wants to be your very close friend. For that to happen, you will need to spend time together. You can spend time with God by reading his Word, the Bible. You can ask your parents to help you know where and how to read. Also, you can talk with God about your life (called praying). When you pray, tell God about your fears and hopes. Thank him for loving you. Tell him that you are sorry for disobeying him, and ask him to help you to get closer to him and do what he wants. You can also tell him about other people and their problems, asking him to help those people, too.

You also get closer to God through worship. That's why churches have worship services. There, with other Christians, you can sing praises to God, talk to him, think about him, remember how much he loves you and what Jesus did for you, and learn from his Word.

Remember that God will draw closer to you if you draw closer to him. Tell him you want to get to know him better. Ask him to draw you closer to himself. You can't get closer to God just by doing a few "Christian" things. But you can get closer to him by having a relationship with him and asking him to help you get to know him better!

---

**KEY VERSE:** *When you draw close to God, God will draw close to you. Wash your hands, sinners! Let your hearts be filled with God. He will make them pure and true to him. (James 4:8)*

**RELATED VERSES:** *Colossians 1:9-14; 1 Thessalonians 5:17; 2 Timothy 3:16-17*

# Q: IF LYING IS A SIN, WHY DID SOME PEOPLE IN THE BIBLE TELL LIES?

## 16

**A:** It is true that the Bible has stories about people who told lies, but the huge majority of Bible people told the truth. God never says in the Bible that lying is right. Some people in the Bible chose to lie, but God didn't say they were good for doing that. God is truth, and he wants us to tell the truth. Honesty is very important for families, neighborhoods, cities, schools, companies, and friendships. Honesty protects us from danger and helps us to be happier people. Be someone who always tells the truth, because that's how God is.

**KEY VERSE:** *Stop lying to each other. Tell the truth. We are part of each other. So when we lie to each other we are hurting ourselves. (Ephesians 4:25)*

**RELATED VERSES:** *Proverbs 6:16-17; 26:18-19; John 8:44; 14:6*

**RELATED QUESTIONS:** *Is it ever OK to break a promise or tell a lie? What about Jacob in the Bible? Why do people in the Bible kill people? Is it OK to lie if God told you to?*

**NOTE TO PARENTS:** *One of the reasons for the stories in the Bible is so we can learn from the examples, both good and bad, of the people in them. Some of their choices set good examples, and some set bad ones. We shouldn't follow every example in the Bible. The fact that Samson lied doesn't mean we should. Whenever you read Bible stories about such people, ask, "What did this person do that was right?" and, "What did this person do that was wrong?"*

# TRUTH
## OR
# CONSEQUENCES

**WHY DOES GOD HAVE RULES?**

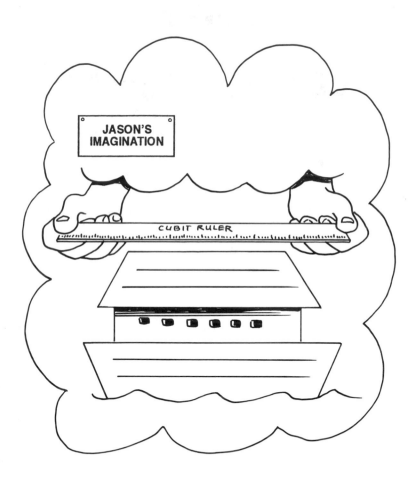

## 17

**A:** God has rules to protect us and to help us. In one way, God's rules are like a wall that protects us from danger. The wall stops us from going any further than we should and getting into trouble. Although we don't always know what is on the other side of the wall, God does, and he loves us so much that he wants to keep us away from it.

God also has rules to help us grow and become all that he wants us to be. Think of feeding a baby. The baby may not like the food—the way it looks, tastes, and feels—but we know that he or she needs to eat good food in order to be healthy and to grow. Like the baby, we don't know everything we need, but God does. In order to help us, he tells us what to do.

God loves us more than anyone else does, and he knows what is best for us. His rules are for our benefit. That's why we need to trust him and obey him.

---

**KEY VERSES:** *Until Christ came we were guarded by the law. We were kept by the law until we could believe in the coming Savior. Let me put it another way. The Jewish laws were our teacher and guide until Christ came. He gave us right standing with God through our faith. (Galatians 3:23-24)*

**RELATED VERSES:** *Deuteronomy 5:31-33; 7:8; Psalm 19:7-11; 119:9, 33-40; Romans 2:20; 7:12; Hebrews 12:9-11*

**RELATED QUESTION:** *Why are there so many laws in the Bible?*

# Q: WHY DOESN'T GOD WANT US TO HAVE FUN?

## 18

**A:** If people think or say that God doesn't want us to have fun, they don't know the truth about God. He *does* want us to have fun. Jesus was happy, and he told people that they would find joy by following him. Also, God tells us in the Bible that heaven is a place of nonstop joy.

Doing what is wrong (sinning) can be fun, but the fun doesn't last, and it leads to bad consequences. It's like eating something that tastes good but that makes you sick later. The main reason we shouldn't sin is that God tells us not to, and we need to trust him. God knows us better than anyone else does. His fun and joy and happiness are the greatest! And they last forever!

Nobody can have more fun than people who know God. You don't have to sin to have fun.

---

**KEY VERSE:** *I have told you this so that you will be filled with my joy. (John 15:11)*

**RELATED VERSES:** *Psalm 5:11; 19:8; Luke 10:21; John 3:29; 17:13; Romans 14:17; Galatians 5:22; Philippians 1:25; Hebrews 11:24-25; Jude 1:24*

**RELATED QUESTION:** *Does the Lord have hate in him?*

**NOTE TO PARENTS:** *Be careful not to imply that people who sin aren't having fun. Kids know better, from observation and from their own experience! Emphasize the fact that God's way is the best way for us, even though another way may seem better. Also, make the distinction between immediate pleasure and a joyful, healthy life.*

## 19

**A:** God is very sad when we do bad things. In fact, he is more upset and grieved over the sins of the world than anyone else. God is sad because he sees how much sin hurts us and others. But God realizes that we are growing and we make mistakes sometimes. He keeps on encouraging us. He loves us so much that he will not give up on us.

**KEY VERSE:** *Don't cause the Holy Spirit sorrow by the way you live. Remember, he has marked you until the day when salvation will be complete. (Ephesians 4:30)*

**RELATED VERSES:** *2 Samuel 24:16; Matthew 23:37*

**RELATED QUESTIONS:** *What does it mean to grieve the Holy Spirit? What if I didn't believe in the Bible? Does Jesus really love me?*

**NOTE TO PARENTS:** *Some parents use this truth to get children to behave. But many children, especially younger ones, already feel guilty about their wrongdoing and will be oversensitive to the idea that they have hurt God's feelings. Instead, tell them that God loves them, is helping them to be good, and is very pleased when they do the right thing!*

# Q: HOW DO YOU GET PERMISSION TO GO TO HEAVEN?

## 20

**A:** There is only one way to get to heaven, and that is through Jesus Christ. Only people who trust in Jesus go to heaven. We can place our trust in Jesus by praying to God and telling him that

1. we are sorry for our sins—for disobeying him and living only for ourselves;
2. we believe that Jesus, his only Son, came to earth and died on the cross, in our place, to take the punishment for our sin, and that he rose again from the dead; and
3. we want his Holy Spirit to live inside us and guide us.

The Bible says that whoever does this and means it becomes a new person, a child of God. And all of God's children will go to be with him in heaven when they die.

---

**KEY VERSE:** *God loved the world so much that he gave his only Son. Anyone who believes in him will not die but have eternal life. (John 3:16)*

**RELATED VERSES:** *Matthew 7:21; John 1:11-13; 14:6; Romans 10:9-10*

**RELATED QUESTIONS:** *Am I a bad person if I don't ask Jesus into my heart? How does God choose who goes to heaven?*

**NOTE TO PARENTS:** *Leading your son or daughter to Christ can arise quite easily out of discussions about right and wrong. Be ready for it by knowing what to say when a child asks a question such as this one.*

# Q: IF YOU SWEAR AND YOU'RE A CHRISTIAN, DO YOU STILL GO TO HEAVEN?

## 21

**A:** If we have given our lives to Christ, we will go to heaven, even if we occasionally do something bad (such as swear). But our relationship with God will affect the way we live. People will be able to see a difference in our lives because we are Christians. Yes, we can do bad things and still go to heaven, but why would we want to? God wants only the very best for us, and sinning hurts us.

Heaven is a place where everyone does good all the time. That's because heaven is perfect and God is there. People who love God love doing good. If we love God, we will want to please him, and we will trust that he knows what's best for us.

**KEY VERSE:** *Now is the time to throw away anger, hatred, cursing, and dirty language. (Colossians 3:8)*

**RELATED VERSES:** *Proverbs 4:24; Romans 8:38-39; 1 Peter 1:15-16*

**RELATED QUESTIONS:** *If I ask Jesus into my heart and then do bad stuff, will I go to hell? If you lied and then died before asking forgiveness, would you still go to heaven? Will I go to hell if I backslide? If you drink and drive and crash and die, do you still go to heaven? If you sin every minute, will you still go to heaven?*

**NOTE TO PARENTS:** *This question will usually arise out of what kids hear from adults, not just their peers. If you hear your child using swear words, take the opportunity to explain that it is wrong and why it is wrong. Also keep in mind that what you model pulls a lot of weight. If you swear, so will your kids.*

# Q: WHY DO I FEEL BAD WHEN I DO SOMETHING WRONG?

## 22

**A:** When we do something wrong, we may feel bad because it hurts others. Or we may feel frustrated because we didn't do what was best. Also, we may feel guilty because we have let God down.

God wants us to do right, so he built a warning system in us to alert us when we are about to do something wrong. That warning system is called a *conscience*. If we get too close to a fire, the heat warns us to move away before we get hurt. Our conscience warns us that doing bad things will hurt us if we do them.

---

**KEY VERSES:** *I am no longer sorry that I sent that letter to you. I was very sorry for a time. I knew how much it would hurt you. But it hurt you only for a little while. Now I am glad I sent it. Not because it hurt you but because the pain turned you to God. It was a good kind of sadness you felt. It was the kind of sadness God wants his people to have. So I don't need to come to you and be rough. God sometimes uses sadness to help us turn away from sin and seek eternal life. We should never be angry that he has sent it. But the sadness of the man who is not a Christian doesn't change him. It brings him more death. (2 Corinthians 7:8-10)*

**RELATED VERSES:** *Acts 24:16; Romans 2:15; 1 Corinthians 4:4; 1 Peter 3:16*

**RELATED QUESTIONS:** *Why do I feel guilty? What is guilt?*

**NOTE TO PARENTS:** *There's a difference between guilt feelings and a true sense of wrong. Some children are supersensitive and feel guilty about almost everything they do. If that describes your child, help him or her understand the depth of God's love and forgiveness.*

# Q: WHAT DOES GOD WANT ME TO DO WHEN I DO SOMETHING WRONG?

## 23

**A:** The first thing we should do is to pray and admit to God what we have done. We should tell him that we are sorry and that we want him to help us not to do it again. Also, we should ask God to help us learn from the experience. Admitting our sins to God brings us back close to him. Remember, God wants to protect us and to provide all we need for living. So we should stay close to him and talk with him about everything. Try praying when you first think of doing something wrong. God can help you avoid or get out of trouble.

If our sin has hurt others, we should talk to them, too, saying we're sorry and asking for their forgiveness.

---

**KEY VERSE:** *If we confess our sins, he can be depended on to forgive us. He will cleanse us from every wrong. It is proper for God to do this because Christ died for our sins. (1 John 1:9)*

**RELATED VERSES:** *Matthew 5:23-24*

**RELATED QUESTIONS:** *Is it wrong to not confess something I did wrong? Do I have to do everything right?*

**NOTE TO PARENTS:** *If your child comes to you with a confession, see it as a teachable moment—help the child see what can be learned from it. Be gentle, loving, and forgiving; otherwise the child may be unwilling to come to you again. Often children are strapped with guilt. If so, consider rituals that can help free them from it, such as writing down their sins on a piece of paper, talking with God about them, and then tearing up the paper together.*

# TELLING
## THE
# TRUTH

# Q: IS IT ALL RIGHT TO TELL A LIE ONCE IN A WHILE?

## 24

**A:** We should always tell the truth because God always tells the truth. Would it be all right to touch a hot stove every once in a while? If you did, you would burn yourself every time. It is never right to lie, not even once in a while. God tells us to tell the truth because he is truth.

Lying also gets us into trouble. Usually one lie leads to another. It's so much simpler to tell the truth than to have to remember the lies we have told so that we can keep them covered up. And lying makes it hard for others to trust us. But people who are honest are free and joyful.

---

**KEY VERSE:** *Stop lying to each other. Tell the truth. We are part of each other. So when we lie to each other we are hurting ourselves. (Ephesians 4:25)*

**RELATED VERSES:** *Exodus 20:16; 1 Corinthians 13:6; 2 Corinthians 4:2; Titus 1:2; Hebrews 6:18*

**RELATED QUESTIONS:** *Is there such a thing as a white lie? Is it wrong to tell your parents that your brother did it when he really didn't? Why is it wrong to lie?*

**NOTE TO PARENTS:** *Your example is going to make a big difference here. How do you represent the truth? How you represent the truth will guide them more than the answer you provide to a question about lying. When you catch children lying, find out why they lied, point out the mistake in their reasoning, and show why the truth would work better.*

## 25

**A:** No. Lying is wrong because God is truth and because he has told us not to lie. Telling the truth can be difficult at times, especially when we might get embarrassed or punished for doing so. But we should do what is right even when it's not easy. Doing it God's way is better in the long run.

Actually, although lying is common, people want others to be truthful with them. If you tell the truth when it's hard, people will think, *Wow!* They will really respect you. They will come to trust you and learn that you are a dependable person. They may even look to you for advice and leadership. Get into the habit of telling the truth. Very few people will stop being your friend just because you tell the truth. Your friends, classmates, relatives, and neighbors want to be able to trust what you say. The truth helps you; lies get you into even more trouble.

---

**KEY VERSES:** *[Jesus] never sinned. He never told a lie. He never answered back when insulted. When he suffered he did not threaten to get even. He left his case in the hands of God who always judges fairly. (1 Peter 2:22-23)*

**RELATED VERSES:** *Genesis 20:1-18; 26:1-11; Exodus 20:16; Mark 14:53-65; James 5:12; 1 Peter 2:1*

**RELATED QUESTIONS:** *Is it OK if I broke someone's window with my ball when I was playing with my dog and didn't tell them? Is it wrong to lie so I don't get into trouble?*

**NOTE TO PARENTS:** *Children sometimes face embarrassing situations in school—situations that tempt them to lie to save face or to improve their image. At times like that, encourage them to trust in God and in his protection.*

# Q: IS IT OK FOR MOM AND DAD TO LIE TO YOU ABOUT YOUR CHRISTMAS PRESENTS?

## 26

**A:** God wants us always to be truthful. But that doesn't mean that we have to answer every question that people ask us, nor does it mean that we have to tell them everything we know. If you ask your parents, "What did you get me for Christmas?" or "Did you get me a bike for Christmas?" they can say something like: "I'm not going to tell you because I want you to be surprised."

Be careful not to make excuses for lying. Don't lie and then make up a reason for doing it. When it comes to giving gifts, there are ways to surprise people and make them feel special without lying to them.

---

**KEY VERSE:** *Most of all, brothers, don't swear by Heaven or earth or anything else. Just say a simple yes or no. That way you won't sin and be guilty for it. (James 5:12)*

**RELATED VERSES:** *Exodus 20:16; Proverbs 22:11; Colossians 4:6*

**RELATED QUESTION:** *Is it OK to lie if you are trying not to hurt people?*

**NOTE TO PARENTS:** *Children often don't make allowances for "socially acceptable" lies the way some adults do. And that's good! Make it a household rule always to speak the truth. Your commitment to truth telling will have the benefit of developing honesty in your child.*

# Q: IF I BREAK SOMETHING THAT BELONGS TO SOMEONE ELSE BUT FIX IT, DO I HAVE TO TELL WHAT I DID?

## 27

**A:** How would *you* feel if a friend broke something of yours and didn't tell you, even though your friend fixed it? You probably wouldn't like it, especially if you found out later. Treating another person the way you want to be treated is called the Golden Rule. Jesus taught that this is the way we should always act.

Telling the person what you did is both telling the truth and showing that you respect that person. If you break something that belongs to someone else, it *is* important to fix it or to pay to have it fixed. But you should let the person know what you did and not try to hide it.

When you do that, people will know you are responsible, and they will let you borrow other things and trust you more. But if you try to hide it and they find out, they won't trust you anymore.

---

**KEY VERSE:** *Do for others what you want them to do for you. This is the meaning of the laws of Moses and the words of the prophets. (Matthew 7:12)*

**RELATED VERSES:** *Exodus 20:16; 22:14*

**NOTE TO PARENTS:** *Many children lie for reasons that are related to self-doubt and insecurity. They lie to show off or because of fear—fear of being thought less of, fear of failure (they lie to seem to have succeeded), fear of not being accepted, and fear of getting punished. Help your child to see that God can protect us from these fears when we respect others and their property. If you get a gratuitous confession of wrongdoing, accept it lovingly, with gentleness. This will encourage your child to tell the truth instead of being afraid of punishment.*

## 28

**A:** All people sin, and one of the most common sins is lying. In fact, some people don't know the difference between truth and lies because they lie so much. Some are so confused that they think a lie is the truth. But not all people lie. Lying is a choice.

Sometimes people say something that is not true because they don't know all the facts; that's not the same as lying. For example, they might say, "Jimmy is in the backyard," when actually he came inside a few minutes ago. It's good to check the facts to make sure that what you say is correct. Watch out for saying something before you're sure it's true.

People who want to do things God's way make a decision not to lie, because they want to obey God. Jesus never lied. If we do lie, we must ask God for forgiveness, admit our lie to the people involved, and try not to do it again.

---

**KEY VERSE:** *Yes, all have sinned. All fall short of God's perfect glory. (Romans 3:23)*

**RELATED VERSES:** *Psalm 14:2-3; Proverbs 18:17; 19:5, 9; Romans 3:10-18; Ephesians 4:19-25*

**RELATED QUESTION:** *Why do people lie?*

**NOTE TO PARENTS:** *It's confusing for children when they hear something that later turns out to be false information and think that they have been lied to. Instead of knowingly telling a lie, however, the person may simply have been passing on misinformation. Use this fact of life to warn your children against accusing someone of being a liar, and encourage them to be careful about what they themselves say. For example, they could say, "I'm not sure, but I think . . ."*

# Q: IS IT WRONG TO TELL SOME-ONE YOUR PARENTS ARE HOME WHEN THEY'RE NOT?

MY PARENTS ARE TIED UP AT THE MOMENT COULD I HAVE THEM RETURN YOUR CALL?

## 29

A: Telling someone that your parents are home when they aren't is a lie, and God tells us not to lie. If we tell this kind of lie, we will find it easier to lie about other things. But that doesn't mean you have to answer every question that a stranger on the phone asks you. If you are home alone, you probably shouldn't tell people on the phone that your parents aren't home. Instead, you could say something like: "They can't come to the phone right now," or, "They are not available," or, "Please let me take a message, and they will get right back to you." Talk with your mom or dad about what you can say without lying.

---

**KEY VERSE:** *A good person is known by his truthfulness. A false person is known by his cheating and lies. (Proverbs 12:17)*

**RELATED VERSES:** *Proverbs 14:15; Ephesians 5:6-10*

**RELATED QUESTION:** *Would it be wrong to lie to someone to protect your parents' belongings?*

**NOTE TO PARENTS:** *Telling the truth doesn't mean telling everything you know about something. Telling everything you know may be more than the person could understand or may simply not be appropriate. Help your child understand that you can withhold information without lying. You can say, "I can't tell you," or, "I'm not going to tell you," or, "I can't explain it right now." Just because you want them to withhold certain facts doesn't mean they have to say something false. Help kids learn the difference between handling information wisely and lying.*

# Q: IS IT OK TO LIE, KNOWING YOU WILL TELL THE TRUTH LATER?

## 30

**A:** One of the most common excuses for lying is, "I was going to tell the truth later." That may sound all right, but usually it is just another lie.

This often happens when people are joking around. They make up a story for the sake of making people laugh. It's OK to joke and to kid around, but it's not OK to lie. Be careful not to make an excuse for lying by saying, "It was just a joke," or, "I was going to tell the truth later." If you do, after a while people won't know when you're telling the truth and when you're not, and they might stop trusting you.

The second most important thing in life is our relationships with others, and one of the most important parts of a good relationship is trust. No joke is more important than that.

---

**KEY VERSES:** *A person might be caught lying to his neighbor. And he might say, "I was just fooling." But if he does this, he is like a madman throwing around firebrands, arrows, and death! (Proverbs 26:18-19)*

**RELATED VERSE:** *Ephesians 4:25*

**RELATED QUESTION:** *Is it wrong to pull pranks?*

**NOTE TO PARENTS:** *Parents tend to justify lies by saying, "This person can't handle the truth." If you want to keep some truths or pieces of the truth from kids, then say the parts that you can tell, or say nothing. Sometimes parents make up lies to motivate kids to do certain undesirable things ("Eat your bread crusts because they'll make your hair curly"). Think of good ways to motivate without resorting to lies.*

# Q: IS IT OK TO LIE TO KEEP A FRIEND FROM GETTING HURT?

## 31

# A:

We don't have to lie to keep our friends from getting hurt. We can think of better ways. For example, depending on the situation, we can get the help of an adult who knows the friend and cares about him or her, or we can say to the friend, "I'm not going to tell you because I don't want you to get hurt." There are many other ways to help a friend besides lying.

God loves you and wants you to be truthful. So he won't force you to lie or put you in a situation where you have to lie. Look for other ways to respond.

Remember that God's way is always the best. You may think that lying will keep someone from getting hurt, but actually it will just make the situation worse.

---

**KEY VERSE:** *Remember, the wrong desires in your life aren't anything new. Many others have faced the same problems before you. You can trust God. He won't let you be carried away by sin. He will show you how to escape. You will survive the test. (1 Corinthians 10:13)*

**RELATED VERSE:** *Ephesians 4:25*

**RELATED QUESTIONS:** *Is it OK to lie if you're going to get hurt? What if a friend has threatened to hurt me if I tell on him, but I know that he is doing something wrong? If you lie for a friend's sake, would it be wrong? Is it wrong not to speak up when someone is being blamed for something he didn't do?*

**NOTE TO PARENTS:** *Beware of talking about hypothetical situations. If your child asks you this kind of question, try to determine what real situation is behind it. Then, together, you can think of a way to help the friend and your child stay out of trouble.*

## 32

**A:** How you respond to a lie depends on who it affects. A friend might lie and say, "I shot twenty free throws in a row without missing." That kind of lie doesn't need any response (in fact, saying nothing is probably best). But if a class partner shows up to give a report with you and says, "I'm all ready" and isn't, that will affect both of you and the class. Or if someone lies to an adult about a situation you were involved in, that will affect both of you and possibly others. In cases like that, you need to respond in some way.

In other words, you can ignore some made-up stories or exaggerations. At other times, however, you should tell the person telling the lie that what he or she is saying just isn't true. This is important when the lie will hurt someone, such as making up a bad story about someone at school, cheating in class, or telling something that isn't true to get money from someone or to get that person to do something wrong.

With very serious lies, you should tell an adult. In these situations, someone could get in big trouble or get hurt badly.

---

**KEY VERSE:** *Brothers, do you know what to do if a Christian is overcome by sin? You who are godly should humbly help him back onto the right path. Remember that next time it might be one of you who sins. (Galatians 6:1)*

**RELATED VERSES:** *Romans 14:16; Ephesians 5:11; Colossians 3:9; 1 Thessalonians 5:11; Hebrews 3:13; 10:24*

# Q: IS IT OK TO KEEP SECRETS FROM YOUR FRIENDS?

## 33

**A:** Most of the time it is all right to keep secrets. Telling the truth doesn't mean that we have to tell *everything* we know to everyone who asks. Sometimes secrets can be fun, like with birthday presents or other pleasant surprises. Sometimes secrets are important because it's better for you not to give out certain information to just anyone.

We should *not* keep something a secret if it means that someone will get hurt or get into serious trouble. For example, a boy might say that he is going to beat up another kid, or a girl might say that she's going to steal something from a store. In those cases, we should tell someone who can help—perhaps a parent, a teacher, a coach, a youth leader, or a school counselor.

Be careful not to promise to keep a secret before you hear what it is. Whether you tell or not should depend on what the secret is.

---

**KEY VERSE:** *Don't tell your secrets to a gossip unless you want them broadcast to the world. (Proverbs 20:19)*

**RELATED VERSES:** *Proverbs 11:13; 27:6; Matthew 6:3-6*

**RELATED QUESTION:** *What do you do when a friend does something you know will hurt them and they said not to tell?*

**NOTE TO PARENTS:** *Encourage your child to tell you if they hear something from a friend that will hurt someone or lead to serious trouble. Let your child know that telling secrets to people who can help in those situations is part of being a good friend. On the other hand, don't encourage "tattling." A tattletale runs and tells adults insignificant things in order to get what they want out of a problem that they could have resolved themselves.*

# Q: SHOULD I TELL THE TRUTH TO SOMEONE EVEN IF THEY WON'T LIKE IT?

## 34

**A:** You should strive to tell the truth, even if it hurts, but never just to be cruel. Here are a few examples to help you decide how to do that.

Sometimes the truth hurts, but we still need to say it. Imagine that a friend asks you to a party. You can't go, but you don't want to hurt your friend's feelings. So you say yes, or you don't say anything and let her think you will be there. Even though your friend will feel bad that you can't come to the party, it would be much better to tell her the truth right away.

Another time you need to tell the unpleasant truth is when a friend is getting into trouble. That friend might be starting to hang around with bad kids. Being a good friend means telling your friend the truth. That friend may not like what you have to say, but it's the truth, and he or she needs to hear it from you.

Being honest and truthful, however, does *not* give us permission to be cruel. Remember, God is loving and kind. So we shouldn't tell people things that will hurt their feelings just because those things are true. It would be cruel, for example, to tell someone, "You have a big nose," or, "You don't play basketball very well," or, "Your house sure needs to be painted," or, "Your clothes are old and worn out."

---

**KEY VERSE:** *We will lovingly follow the truth at all times. We will speak truly, deal truly, and live truly. So we will become more in every way like Christ. He is the Head of his body, the Church. (Ephesians 4:15)*

**RELATED VERSES:** *2 Samuel 12:1-12; 2 Kings 5:1-14; Proverbs 27:6*

# Q: IF YOU DON'T LIKE SOMETHING A PERSON WEARS AND THEY ASK YOU IF YOU LIKE IT, ARE YOU SUPPOSED TO TELL THEM THE TRUTH?

## 35

**A:** We are not supposed to lie, but that doesn't mean that we have to be mean or hurtful about what we say. We need to learn *tact*. Tact is telling the truth in a nice way, even if it's hard for the other person to take. For example, suppose you think a person's new coat is ugly. You don't have to say, "I *hate* that ugly coat!" You can think of something good about it, like, "It looks nice and warm." Practice saying what you think in ways that respect people's feelings.

---

**KEY VERSE:** *We will lovingly follow the truth at all times. We will speak truly, deal truly, and live truly. So we will become more in every way like Christ. He is the Head of his body, the Church. (Ephesians 4:15)*

**RELATED VERSE:** *Luke 6:31*

**RELATED QUESTION:** *Is it OK to lie to people about how they look just to be nice?*

**NOTE TO PARENTS:** *This may be the time to explain the difference between lying and being tactful. Lying is an attempt to deceive or to trick someone. Tact is an attempt to be kind in the delivery of a truth that may offend someone. Also, teach your child not to go to the other extreme: Flattery is equally wrong—and can be itself a form of lying. We should never lie just because it will make someone feel good. Rather, we should always deliver the truth in a loving way.*

# SCHOOL DAYS
## DAYS
### AND
# TV DAZE

# Q: IS IT WRONG TO WATCH MUSIC VIDEOS?

PROTECTIVE GLASSES

MUSIC VIDEOS UP NEXT

## 36

**A:** It's not wrong to watch television, listen to the radio, watch videos, or listen to music. But God wants us to be wise about what we put into our minds. A lot of the stuff on TV, in movies, in videos, and on talk radio is not good. In fact, often the people on them use bad language, do bad things, and make it look as if sinning is the right thing to do. That's a lie. We know that God wants us to do what is right, not wrong. He doesn't want us to disobey him. So we should be very careful about what we watch and listen to. Many music videos are not good. Seeing and hearing bad videos is like eating garbage. It's bad for us, won't help us grow, and will make us sick. Instead, we should fill our minds with pictures, words, and thoughts that honor God.

---

**KEY VERSE:** *And now, brothers, as I close this letter, let me say one more thing. Fix your thoughts on what is true and good and right. Think about things that are pure and lovely. Dwell on the fine, good things in others. Think about all you can praise God for and be glad about. (Philippians 4:8)*

**RELATED VERSE:** *Ephesians 5:11*

**RELATED QUESTIONS:** *Why are some music videos so stupid? Why is it wrong to watch music videos?*

**NOTE TO PARENTS:** *Beware of making a sweeping statement against music videos. Some Christian musicians make music videos. Beware of making sweeping statements against anything in youth culture. As you and your children confront new challenges, learn to compare them to God's standards.*

# Q: WHY DO SOME PEOPLE MAKE MUSIC WITH BAD WORDS?

## 37

**A:** Some music writers and performers have no hope and don't love God, so they write and sing angry and hateful songs. Other music has bad words because the writers and singers want to shock the listeners, to get their attention. Because these musicians don't love God, they think it's all right to use shocking language. Much of the time, however, music has bad words because the writers, singers, producers, and stores want to make money. Unfortunately, that kind of music sells, so they keep making the bad songs.

Don't buy music that has swearing or a false message about life. If a bad song comes on the radio, change the station. Don't fill your mind with garbage.

---

**KEY VERSES:** *People who long to be rich do all kinds of wrong things for money. They do things that hurt them and make them evil-minded. Finally these things send them to hell itself. The love of money is the first step toward all kinds of sin. Some people have even turned away from God because of their love for it. As a result they have pierced themselves with many sorrows. (1 Timothy 6:9-10)*

**RELATED VERSES:** *Proverbs 4:24; Ephesians 4:29; Philippians 4:8*

**RELATED QUESTIONS:** *Why do people make music about the highway to hell? Why do people swear?*

**NOTE TO PARENTS:** *Music itself isn't bad. It's a good thing that some people corrupt. Help your children find music they can enjoy listening to that doesn't violate God's standards.*

# Q: IS IT OK TO LISTEN TO BAD MUSIC GROUPS IF YOU DON'T LISTEN TO THE WORDS?

## 38

**A:** Trying to listen to bad songs without hearing the words would be like trying to watch a video with your eyes closed. It can't be done. Even if you aren't concentrating on the words, you still hear them and they affect your thoughts. Also, imagine what others would think of you if they saw and heard you listening to music that *they* know is bad. They probably would wonder what kind of Christian you were. Also, buying and listening to music supports the musicians who perform it, and you don't want to support the bad groups.

But not all music is bad! Many songs are fun to listen to, and they have good words. Fill your mind with what is good—do everything to the glory of God. Trust that the things God approves are the best for you. He loves you!

---

**KEY VERSE:** *You must do everything for God's glory, even your eating and drinking. (1 Corinthians 10:31)*

**RELATED VERSES:** *Romans 12:2; Philippians 4:8*

**RELATED QUESTIONS:** *Is it wrong to listen to secular music? Is it wrong to listen to secular music if you read the lyrics and they aren't that bad?*

**NOTE TO PARENTS:** *Music matters a great deal to most older kids and to their relationships. It's OK to limit what your children can listen to, but it will be more effective to steer kids instead of blocking them. In other words, when you say that they can't listen to a certain group, suggest alternatives. Don't give them the impression that the only good music is the stuff that you listen to (or listened to when you were their age).*

# Q: WHY DON'T YOU LET US WATCH CERTAIN TV SHOWS?

## 39

**A:** Many TV programs show people saying and doing things that go against God and what he says. Many of the people who make television shows aren't Christians. They don't know God and will often make programs that are not good for us to watch. Some shows even encourage us to do wrong things. We should always try to do what is right. So it is good to turn off the set or change the channel when a bad show comes on. We should guard our hearts, because what we put into our hearts will show up in our lives (Proverbs 4:23).

**KEY VERSE:** *And now, brothers, as I close this letter, let me say one more thing. Fix your thoughts on what is true and good and right. Think about things that are pure and lovely. Dwell on the fine, good things in others. Think about all you can praise God for and be glad about. (Philippians 4:8)*

**RELATED VERSES:** *Proverbs 4:23; 23:7; Ephesians 5:11; Philippians 2:14-16; James 4:4*

**RELATED QUESTIONS:** *Why does what you watch on TV matter if you're a Christian? Why do we have to be careful about what we watch on TV? Is it right or wrong to watch worldly movies? Is it bad to watch TV?*

**NOTE TO PARENTS:** *This is the kind of question that touches on the fundamental issue of what we are here for. We are here to learn to love, to learn to trust, to live with God beside us, and to show God's love to others—not to seek immediate personal pleasure. Help your children to see the bigger picture to help them make good choices in individual areas of life.*

# Q: WHAT IF ONE PARENT SAYS YOU CAN WATCH A CERTAIN MOVIE, AND THEN THE OTHER ONE SAYS YOU CAN'T?

## 40

**A:** If one parent tells you no, then accept that as your answer and don't go looking for permission from your other parent. Some kids go back and forth between parents until one gives in and says OK. That's wrong because it dishonors what the first parent said. If Mom or Dad says you can't do something (like watch a certain movie), you may nicely ask why. That will help you understand the reason for the no. But don't argue, complain, or whine about it. Instead, say thank you and obey. God wants us to honor and obey our parents. He told us that in his Word.

Why does God want children to obey their parents? Because that's how God keeps kids safe and gives them what they need to grow up. Obeying and honoring your parents will help you learn the things you need to live a happy and productive life.

---

**KEY VERSES:** *Young person, obey your father and your mother. Take to heart all of their advice. Keep in mind all that they tell you. (Proverbs 6:20-21)*

**RELATED VERSES:** *Exodus 20:12; Ephesians 6:1-3*

**NOTE TO PARENTS:** *It's very important for parents to support each other when kids come to one parent with a request designed to undo what the other said. Make it a policy to enforce the first answer as the final answer unless you both agree to change your mind.*

## 41

# A:

Some jokes are funny but not good. We should avoid laughing at dirty jokes. A "dirty" joke uses foul words or talks about sex in a wrong way, just to get a laugh. It is called a dirty joke, even by people who don't know God, because it's bad. Jokes that make fun of other people, their race, skin color, religion, and so forth are also bad. Why? Because God is holy and pure and he wants us to be pure. Being like him is the key to living the way he meant us to live. Telling or listening to dirty jokes fills our mind with wrong thoughts and may cause others to feel bad.

If you are near someone who is telling jokes that are bad, go away from that person. You don't want to listen to the jokes, and you don't want to encourage the person who is telling them. There are plenty of good, clean jokes. Listen to those, tell those, and have fun!

---

**KEY VERSE:** *Dirty stories, foul talk, and coarse jokes are not for you. Instead, remind each other of God's goodness and be thankful. (Ephesians 5:4)*

**RELATED VERSES:** *Exodus 23:2; Psalm 1:1-2; Proverbs 3:32; 4:14-15*

**RELATED QUESTIONS:** *Is it OK to laugh at funny jokes about bad things? Is it wrong to tell bad jokes?*

**NOTE TO PARENTS:** *It is amazing what we will compromise because something makes us laugh. Be careful not to repeat or laugh at dirty jokes. Humor is not trivial. And to a child, laughter represents approval.*

# Q:
## IS IT WRONG TO LEAVE YOUR HOMEWORK TILL THE LAST MINUTE SO THAT YOU CAN WATCH TV?

## 42

A: School is important because that's where we learn important information that can help us live in this world. Homework is an important part of school. Teachers give homework to help students learn what is being taught in class. Remember, God wants us to do our best at everything we do—that includes school. TV is all right (if we watch good programs), but school is more important.

To get the most out of school, do your homework first, and do the best you can at it. Family jobs and responsibilities should come before play and entertainment. Then, if you have time, you can take time for playing, watching TV, and other activities. You will often enjoy your relaxation, entertainment, and playtime more after you have completed your responsibilities!

---

**KEY VERSES:** *Take a lesson from the ants, you lazy fellow. Learn from their ways and be wise! They have no king to make them work. But they work hard all summer. They gather food for the winter. (Proverbs 6:6-8)*

**RELATED VERSES:** *Colossians 3:23-24; 1 Timothy 4:12; 2 Timothy 2:15, 22*

**NOTE TO PARENTS:** *You can use this kind of question as an opportunity to talk about responsibility and the satisfaction of a job well done. Everyone has "jobs" to do, and some of them just aren't fun! But we can choose our attitude in every situation, and we can choose to take pleasure in the responsibilities God has given us. Encourage your child not to see work as a drag, but to do it as a service to God and to take pleasure in it.*

# Q: IF YOU SAY **JESUS** WHEN YOU'RE MAD, ISN'T THAT LIKE PRAYING?

## 43

# A:

No. It is one thing to talk to God. It is another to say his name as a swear word because you got hurt or angry.

Sometimes the same word can have different meanings. When and how we say a word can help tell what we mean by it. For example, a person might smile and say, "That's great!" with a happy tone of voice. But another person could frown and mutter angrily, "That's great!" The same words would have very different meanings.

It's the same with God's name. When people use *God, Jesus,* or *Christ* in a sentence, when and how they say those words can tell us what they mean. We pray and worship using God's name. In Sunday school classes we talk a lot about Jesus. And we talk about Christ with our friends. Those are good ways to use God's name. But some people say his name in anger, in frustration, or just in passing. That's called swearing or using God's name "in vain." That's not OK. God says it's wrong.

We love God and want to please him. We love Jesus and thank him for dying on the cross for us. So we should only say *God, Jesus,* or *Christ* when we are being serious about God, praising him, or praying to him. We shouldn't even say "My God!" or "Oh, Lord!" when we're surprised. Treat God with respect. Honor his name. This will show others that you love and respect God, and that will affect them.

---

**KEY VERSE:** *You shall not use the name of the Lord your God irreverently. Nor shall you use it to swear. You will not escape punishment if you do. (Exodus 20:7)*

**RELATED QUESTIONS:** *Why is saying "Oh, my God!" wrong? Why do people say God's name in vain? Is it wrong to swear at other people? Why is it wrong to swear?*

# FAMILY MATTERS

# Q: WHY DO WE HAVE MARRIAGE?

## 44

# A:

God invented marriage because everyone needs someone to be close to and to love and be loved by. He also created marriage as the place for bringing children into the world. Marriage is good. In fact, God brought the first man and woman together in the Garden of Eden before any sin came into the world. God knows what is best for us. He knows that babies and children need a mother and a father to protect them and to care for them. Husbands and wives should stay together, work out their problems, and be good parents. That's God's plan.

---

**KEY VERSE:** *A man should leave his father and mother. And he should be forever united to his wife. (Matthew 19:5)*

**RELATED VERSES:** *Genesis 2:4-25; 1 Corinthians 7:1-2; Ephesians 5:31-33*

**RELATED QUESTION:** *Why do I have to be married to have a baby?*

**NOTE TO PARENTS:** *Emphasize God's role in making families work. God doesn't abandon families that have suffered divorce or other breakdowns. He provided us with marriage; God's plan for a husband and wife is that they will be married for life. In this sinful world, however, divorces do happen. Through his grace, God can make any family the place of protection and provision that kids need. Keep trusting God and depending on him to help you make the most of your situation.*

# Q: ON TV, WHY DO PEOPLE WHO AREN'T MARRIED LIVE TOGETHER?

## 45

**A:** Many of the people who make TV shows don't know God, and they don't care about what God wants. They don't understand that his way is the way that works best. Some television programs try to show that marriage isn't important. But God created marriage, and he says that it *is* important and that it's the right way for a man and a woman to live together.

---

**KEY VERSE:** *Yes, they knew about him. But they wouldn't admit it or worship him. They wouldn't even thank him for all his care for them. They thought up silly ideas about what God was like and what he wanted them to do. So their foolish minds became dark and confused. (Romans 1:21)*

**RELATED VERSES:** *Exodus 20:14, 17; Proverbs 6:25; 7:4-27; Jeremiah 29:6; Malachi 2:14-16; Matthew 19:3-9; Romans 7:2; 1 Corinthians 5:9-11; 6:18-20; 7:8-14; Colossians 3:5; Hebrews 13:4*

**RELATED QUESTIONS:** *When can people do sex? Why is it wrong to have sex before marriage?*

**NOTE TO PARENTS:** *Monitor your family's TV viewing. If you see an inappropriate scene in a program or an advertisement, talk about it with your child. Discuss why it's wrong and what the Bible says about sex.*

# Q: IS KISSING WRONG?

## 46

**A:** Kissing isn't wrong. Many family members kiss each other. In some countries, friends kiss each other on the cheek when they say hello. And husbands and wives also often kiss each other. Kissing is one way that people can show love and affection to the people who are important to them.

---

**KEY VERSES:** *[Jesus] turned to the woman and said to Simon, "Look! See this woman kneeling here! When I came to your home, you didn't offer me water to wash the dust from my feet. But she has washed them with her tears. And she wiped them off with her hair. You did not give me the customary kiss of greeting. But she has kissed my feet from the time I first came in." (Luke 7:44-45)*

**RELATED QUESTION:** *Is it wrong to go out with boys before I'm sixteen?*

**NOTE TO PARENTS:** *Many children try to copy what they see on TV, where kissing happens often. They may be confused and think that kissing is the cool way to express love (or "like") to someone. That's why a boy will sneak up on a girl, kiss her on the cheek, and run away. When young children ask about kissing, take time to explain its proper place and purpose.*

# Q: WHY DO I HAVE TO OBEY MY PARENTS?

**#47**

**A:** The most important reason for children to obey their parents is that God said to. God knows that children need protection and guidance, and parents are the best ones to provide that. Parents take care of their children, give them food and other things they need, and teach them how to know right from wrong. Living God's way means listening to him and doing what he says, and that includes obeying Mom and Dad. Obeying your parents is the best way for you to learn and grow now and to have a better life in the future.

**KEY VERSES:** *Children, obey your parents. This is the right thing to do. Honor your father and mother. This is the first of God's Ten Commandments that ends with a promise. The promise is that you will have a long life, full of blessing. (Ephesians 6:1-3)*

**RELATED VERSES:** *Exodus 20:12; Romans 13:1-7; Colossians 3:20*

**RELATED QUESTIONS:** *Is it wrong for me to argue with my parents? Is it all right to go across the street to your friend's house when your parents want you to do your homework?*

**NOTE TO PARENTS:** *Don't use authority to justify different standards for yourself unless you have a very good reason beyond just the fact that "you're in charge." On the other hand, don't be surprised if your child resists your rules, because kids will protest their parents' decisions no matter how loving and wise they are. To minimize the hassles, always have a good reason for the rules you enforce.*

# Q: IS IT WRONG TO PUT MY FINGERS IN MY EARS SO I CAN'T HEAR MY PARENTS?

## 48

**A:** Some children think that if they can't hear their parents, they don't have to do what their parents tell them. But God tells us to *honor* our parents, not just obey them. That means treating them with respect. When we respect our parents, we look at them when they talk to us, and we listen carefully to what they say—we *don't* try to plug our ears or ignore them. It also means having a good attitude and not talking back. Listening to your parents doesn't just make them feel good—it's for *your* good. God loves you and wants the best for you.

---

**KEY VERSE:** *Honor your father and mother. Do this that you may have a long, good life in the land the Lord your God will give you. (Exodus 20:12)*

**RELATED VERSES:** *Deuteronomy 5:16; Luke 6:31*

**RELATED QUESTIONS:** *Is it wrong to give my parents dirty looks when they're yelling at me? Is it wrong to ignore my parents when they talk if I don't want to listen?*

**NOTE TO PARENTS:** *Don't fall into the trap of yelling to get a child's attention. Often obedience comes more easily if you explain why they are to obey, as well as what you want them to do.*

# Q: WHY IS IT WRONG TO COMPLAIN WHEN MY MOM ASKS ME TO DO SOMETHING?

## 49

**A:** Remember, the Bible tells us to honor our parents. This means being polite, having a good attitude, and showing them respect, even when we disagree with them. If you don't agree with your parents, you can tell them how you feel without complaining or hurting them with words. Also, think about how much they do for you. That will help you have a thankful attitude rather than a complaining one. People who complain a lot don't have many friends, are usually unhappy, and often have miserable lives. And the more they complain, the worse it gets! You can choose to be content and to make the best of every situation.

**KEY VERSE:** *Don't complain or argue in anything you do. (Philippians 2:14)*

**RELATED VERSES:** *Matthew 21:28-31; James 5:9; 1 Peter 4:9*

**RELATED QUESTION:** *Is it all right to complain when my mom asks me to do something?*

**NOTE TO PARENTS:** *Explain to your child: "You don't have to like it; you just have to do it." If your child calmly and respectfully explains his or her objections, affirm the good attitude and consider the objections carefully.*

# Q: IF MY PARENTS ARE ARGUING, IS IT OK TO TELL THEM TO STOP?

## 50

**A:** Sometimes parents disagree, and they need to talk it out. Just because a husband and wife argue doesn't mean they are having serious problems. Even people who love each other deeply will disagree from time to time. Disagreeing isn't wrong, and arguing doesn't mean the people hate each other. Also, it is not your job as a child to see that your parents don't argue. You can tell them how you feel, but don't try to tell them what to do. Pray for your parents if they are arguing. Ask God to help them get along and to give them wisdom for their conversation.

However, if the arguing leads to yelling, screaming, swearing, or hitting, you may have to tell another adult who can help your mom and dad. Your pastor would be a good choice.

---

**KEY VERSE:** *Entering an argument that isn't any of your business is as foolish as yanking a dog's ears. (Proverbs 26:17)*

**RELATED VERSE:** *Philippians 4:2*

**RELATED QUESTIONS:** *If it's wrong to argue, how come my parents do? Do adults always know more than kids?*

**NOTE TO PARENTS:** *Hearing parents argue can be very hard for a child. You and your spouse will disagree and argue from time to time. But be careful about how you argue, especially in front of your children. Fight fairly; that is, don't swear, call the other person names, or use privileged information against him or her. Instead, calm down, lower your voice, acknowledge the other person's position, state your position, and propose a solution. Demonstrate to your children that differences can be resolved peacefully and lovingly.*

# Q: IS IT OK TO TELL SECRETS TO PARENTS?

## 51

**A:** Yes. It is wonderful to have someone you can trust. Mothers and fathers who love their children want to help them every way they can. There is no better person with whom you can share a secret. So it's OK to tell *your own* secrets to your parents. Just be sure to tell them that it's a secret and that you don't want them to tell anybody—then they'll know not to tell. Some children have secrets that they keep from their parents. That is not God's way. How can your parents help you and teach you and take care of you if you don't trust them and talk to them? If someone says you can't tell your parents something, tell them not to tell you, either.

---

**KEY VERSE:** *Don't tell your secrets to a gossip unless you want them broadcast to the world. (Proverbs 20:19)*

**RELATED VERSES:** *Proverbs 11:13; 25:9-10*

**RELATED QUESTION:** *Are there some things I shouldn't tell my parents?*

**NOTE TO PARENTS:** *Children need someone with whom they can share their fears, dreams, and secrets. Your children should always feel confident that they can tell you everything that is on their mind. Guard that information carefully and lovingly. Don't use the information against them, don't belittle what they have shared, and don't betray their trust. Use this opportunity to affirm your children for being honest and for trusting you.*

# Q: IS IT OK TO HIT MY BROTHER BACK IF HE HIT ME FIRST?

## 52

A: No, that would be taking revenge. In the Bible, God says that vengeance, or revenge, belongs to him. And he has delegated the authority to settle fights to the human authorities—police, teachers, and (for brothers and sisters who fight) parents. It's not right to hit back.

God also wants us to love, not hate. If we say we love him but hate people, then we don't really love him. That's because if we can't love someone in our own family, whom we can see, we can't possibly love God, whom we cannot see. That's why Jesus told us to be kind and to respond with love, even when someone hits us.

So if your brother (or sister) hits you, respond by being nice. If he or she continues to be mean, tell your parents and let them take care of it. God wants you to learn how to get along with people. Sometimes that can be very difficult at home. But if you can learn to love and to be kind to your family members, you probably will be able to get along with almost anyone else.

***

**KEY VERSES:** *Never pay back evil for evil. Do things in a way that everyone can see you are honest. (Romans 12:17)*

**RELATED VERSES:** *Matthew 5:9; Romans 12:14; 13:1-7; 1 John 2:9-11; 3:11-15*

**NOTE TO PARENTS:** *One of your challenges as a parent involves teaching kids to talk out their differences rather than fight. You can use a question like this one to emphasize the importance of being a peacemaker. Don't allow your kids to fight, or that is how they will learn to solve problems. Instead, encourage them to talk through their differences, and they will gain valuable skills in working through all sorts of conflicts.*

# Q: IS IT OK TO BUG MY SISTER?

## 53

**A:** God wants us to be kind and considerate; respectful, not mean. Sometimes we may be having fun teasing or tickling each other, but we should stop if the person asks us to. We should not be cruel.

Sometimes we may bug other people by accident. In other words, we may do something that bothers people or makes them angry with us, and we don't even know it. As soon as we find out, we should stop doing it. That would be kind and considerate.

It's easy for brothers and sisters to get on each other's nerves. That's because they spend so much time together and because what one person does affects other people in a family. We need to work hard to make our families places of love and kindness.

---

**KEY VERSE:** *Let's not look for honors or try to be popular. These things make people jealous and cause hard feelings. (Galatians 5:26)*

**RELATED VERSES:** *Genesis 21:9-11; Romans 12:9-10; Galatians 6:10; 1 John 2:9-11*

**RELATED QUESTIONS:** *Is fighting with your brother wrong? Why is it wrong to fight?*

**NOTE TO PARENTS:** *When your children are bothering one another, remember to teach both children the correct response. The person doing the bothering should stop when asked and apologize. But the person being bothered should also try to be more patient.*

# Q: DO I REALLY HAVE TO EAT MY VEGETABLES, OR ARE MY PARENTS JUST MAKING SURE I CLEAN MY PLATE?

## 54

**A:** God has said that children must obey their parents. So even if you don't like the taste of some food, you should eat it if your parents tell you to. Parents serve vegetables and tell children to eat them because vegetables help build strong bodies. The Bible tells us that we should take care of our bodies because that's where God lives and because God wants to use us. We should do what we can to stay healthy. That means eating good food, including vegetables.

---

**KEY VERSE:** *Don't you know that your body is the home of the Holy Spirit? The Holy Spirit lives within you! Your own body does not belong to you. (1 Corinthians 6:19)*

**RELATED VERSES:** *Ephesians 6:1-3*

**RELATED QUESTION:** *Is it OK to throw out the lunch your mom made and go to the store?*

**NOTE TO PARENTS:** *Make good and healthy rules for eating and be very consistent in enforcing them. This brings peace and minimizes arguing because your child knows where the boundaries are. Be careful not to make too big a deal about food rules, though; eating should be a pleasant experience.*

# FRIENDS
## AND
# ENEMIES

# Q: CAN YOU HAVE MORE THAN ONE BEST FRIEND?

## 55

**A:** God wants us to be loving and kind to all people. If you are doing that, you probably will know many kids who like you and want to be your friend. Friends are great, and it's fun to have a lot of them. You can have many good friends, and you don't have to put them in order of who's best. You may have one or two friends who are closer than all the others. But be careful about saying that one person is your *very best* friend. That may make the others feel bad. And don't say that one person is your "best friend" just to make another friend angry or jealous or because you want to exclude the other person.

You can have a favorite food, but you don't *have* to have a best friend. You can be the best kind of friend to many people.

---

**KEY VERSE:** *Always try to be kind to others. Especially be kind to other Christians. (Galatians 6:10)*

**RELATED VERSE:** *Proverbs 17:17*

**RELATED QUESTION:** *What if somebody wants to be my best friend but I don't want to be theirs?*

**NOTE TO PARENTS:** *Encourage your children to be loyal friends, respectful of others' feelings and preferences. Caution them about describing any of their friends as "best friends" if they have other friends who may feel hurt by not having that title. Encourage them to concentrate on being a best friend rather than on getting a best friend. Everything the Bible says about loving others applies to friendship.*

# Q: HOW CAN I LOVE MY ENEMIES?

## 56

**A:** By doing kind things for them, wishing them well, and praying for them. Loving your enemies also means forgiving them and not condemning them. It means that rather than fighting back or trying to hurt them, you treat them like a friend.

If you think that sounds hard to do, you're right! Enemies don't like us and are out to hurt us. They may push us, hit us, call us names, and try to get us into trouble. We don't have to like what they do to us. But with the help of God's Holy Spirit, we can love *them*. After all, that's what God did for us.

God can do anything—even change people. Who knows—today's enemies may turn out to be tomorrow's friends.

---

**KEY VERSES:** *Love your enemies! Do good to them! Lend to them! And don't worry about the fact that they won't pay you back. Then your reward from Heaven will be very great. And you will truly be acting like sons of God. For he is kind to the unthankful and those who are wicked. Try to show as much mercy as your Father does. Never criticize or condemn. If you do, it will all come back on you. Go easy on others. Then they will do the same for you. (Luke 6:35-37)*

**RELATED VERSES:** *Romans 12:17-21*

**RELATED QUESTION:** *What should I do about the bullies at school?*

**NOTE TO PARENTS:** *Every conflict with others is an opportunity for us to learn how to love. Encourage your child to turn conflicts into opportunities to be friendly and loving toward others.*

# Q: IS IT WRONG TO HATE PEOPLE IF THEY'RE NERDS?

## 57

**A:** Yes. Some people are given names like *nerd* or *jerk* for no good reason. Instead of believing the bad things we hear about others, we should think the best of them and try to get to know them.

Even when we meet people who really are "jerks"— who say bad things and are mean to us—we should not *hate* them or be mean back to them. God wants us to be loving and kind to others. So we shouldn't hurt others or make fun of them.

**KEY VERSES:** *There is a saying, "Love your friends and hate your enemies." But I [Jesus] say love your enemies, too! Pray for those who treat you badly! (Matthew 5:43-44)*

**RELATED VERSES:** *Matthew 5:21-22; Luke 6:27-35; Romans 12:17-21*

**RELATED QUESTIONS:** *Is it OK to make fun of someone from a different country? Why does someone feel hurt when I laugh at them?*

**NOTE TO PARENTS:** *This touches on the issue of prejudice. You need to teach your child to respect all people regardless of race, nationality, religion, or economic class. God created diversity among people; there is no need for us to judge some good and some bad. Set the example: Avoid saying negative or stereotypical things about groups or classes of people.*

# Q: IS IT OK TO STAY UP LATE ON SCHOOL NIGHTS IF YOUR FRIENDS DO?

## 58

**A:** What your friends do does not determine what is wrong and right. Every family has its own rules. It is important for *you* to obey *your* parents. So if your parents tell you to go to bed at a certain time, do it, no matter what your friends do. God has given the responsibility of raising you to your parents, not to your friends.

Your parents have a good reason for not wanting you to stay up late on a school night: You will be sleepy the next day, so you won't do your best in school. Mom and Dad know that, so they insist that you get your rest. They know how important it is for you to do well in school.

Sometimes your parents may let you stay up late, like at a sleep-over at a friend's house on a weekend. So it wouldn't be *wrong* in that situation. But still it may not be the smartest thing to do, especially if you try to stay up all night. It's not good for you. Use your head and get the sleep you need.

---

**KEY VERSE:** *Don't copy the world. Be a different person with a fresh newness in all you do and think. Then you will learn how his ways will really satisfy you. (Romans 12:2)*

**RELATED VERSES:** *Exodus 20:12; Colossians 3:20*

**RELATED QUESTIONS:** *Is it OK to follow what your friends do? How do you deal with peer pressure and still follow the Bible?*

**NOTE TO PARENTS:** *When your children start using the excuse, "But all my friends get to do that," remind them of the reason and the reward for doing the right thing. Encourage your children to set a good example, not copy whatever others do.*

# Q: WHAT'S SO BAD ABOUT WANTING TO WEAR CLOTHES THAT ARE IN STYLE?

## 59

**A:** It's all right to wear nice clothes that are in style. We should take care of ourselves and try to look our best. But we shouldn't think that having the latest clothes will make us happy and help us make friends. And we should remember that wearing nice clothes doesn't make a person nice. It's what's on the inside of the person that really counts.

People who design and make new clothes are trying to make money. So they broadcast very clever ads on TV and radio to make people want to buy their clothes. They change the styles every season and say that everyone should wear the latest style. Often the most stylish clothes are also the most expensive.

Work with your parents to buy what you can afford. God wants us to be content with what we have, so don't think that you have nothing to wear because your clothes are not the very latest style. And God wants us to put him in first place in our lives, so don't make clothes and other things more important than he is.

---

**KEY VERSES:** *Don't worry at all about having enough food and clothing. Why be like the heathen? For they take pride in all these things. And they are very worried about them, too. But your heavenly Father already knows that you need them. Give him first place in your life. Live as he wants you to. Then he will give all these things to you as well. (Matthew 6:31-33)*

**RELATED VERSES:** *Philippians 4:11-12; 1 Timothy 6:8; Hebrews 13:5*

**RELATED QUESTION:** *Is it vain to want to have your hair perfect or wear "in style" clothes?*

**Q:** IF I'M SUPPOSED TO LOVE EVERYBODY, WHY AM I SUPPOSED TO STAY AWAY FROM CERTAIN KIDS?

## 60

**A:** God wants us to be loving and kind to everyone, but that doesn't mean we have to be a close friend to everyone. Some people can be bad influences on us. If we spend too much time with them, we can find ourselves doing what we shouldn't do and getting into trouble.

It is good to want to be a good influence on others. So you can try to be friendly to kids whom others think are bad. But if *they* begin to influence *you*, you will need to back off. Think about where you play with them and what you do. Try bringing them to your house to play or inviting them to church. Your closest friends should be those who help you become a better person—those who have the same attitudes about serving God as you have. Try to be close to kids who love God and want to serve him.

Talk with your parents about this problem. And if they tell you to stay away from certain kids, do what they say. Picking good friends is one way parents can really help you.

---

**KEY VERSE:** *Be with wise people and become wise. Be with evil people and become evil. (Proverbs 13:20)*

**RELATED VERSES:** *Proverbs 27:17; John 17:15-17; 1 Corinthians 5:9-11*

**RELATED QUESTIONS:** *If Christians should love others, why is it wrong to have bad friends? Why is it wrong to have certain friends if God wants us to love everybody?*

**NOTE TO PARENTS:** *Friends can have a powerful influence on kids. It's important for you to monitor your child's friendships and affirm positive relationships that your child has formed.*

# Q: IS IT WRONG TO STOP TELLING MY FRIENDS ABOUT JESUS EVEN WHEN THEY WON'T LISTEN?

## 61

**A:** It is good that you want to tell your friends about Jesus, but it is also good to respect them as people. Sometimes your friends won't seem interested. And sometimes, they may tell you that they don't want to talk about it anymore. When that happens, you need to respect their wishes and stop talking a lot about it. This doesn't mean that they won't learn about Jesus from you. You can always share about what God is doing in your life. And, most important of all, you can live like a Christian. Your friends will notice that you are loving and kind and that you don't do bad things. They will see Jesus in you.

---

**KEY VERSES:** *Don't hide your light! Let it shine for all. Let your good deeds glow for all to see. That way they will praise your heavenly Father. (Matthew 5:15-16)*

**RELATED VERSE:** *Ecclesiastes 3:1*

**RELATED QUESTION:** *Why are some kids embarrassed about believing in Jesus?*

**NOTE TO PARENTS:** *Teach your children how to share their faith, but don't put pressure on them to witness. God wants us to live out our faith and to share experiences as well as the facts. You can pray together with your children for opportunities to tell people about Jesus.*

# Q: IF SOME OF MY FRIENDS ARE DOING SOMETHING THAT I THINK IS BAD, SHOULD I TELL MY PARENTS?

## 62

**A:** Yes. It is good to be able to share with your parents what is going on in your life, especially the things that bother you. It is also good to ask for their advice on what to do in certain situations. And if kids are doing something that will hurt themselves or someone else, then definitely tell your parents. They will know what to do to help.

Don't forget, though, that you yourself can speak with your friends about what they're doing. When you tell your parents, you can tell about what your friends are doing; then explain what *you* are going to do. Don't expect Mom or Dad to jump in every time and come to your rescue.

And finally, don't just tell about the bad things that kids are doing. Tell your mom and dad about the good that your friends do, too.

---

**KEY VERSE:** *Take no part in the worthless pleasures of evil and darkness. Instead, rebuke them and bring them out into the light. (Ephesians 5:11)*

**RELATED VERSES:** *Proverbs 10:17-18; 1 Timothy 5:20*

**RELATED QUESTIONS:** *If someone is picking on my brother, is it OK to defend him? When is it right to tell on other kids?*

**NOTE TO PARENTS:** *Value honesty. Don't overreact if kids tell you about things that surprise you. (Otherwise they may be less likely to share in the future.)*

# Q: IS IT OK TO THINK THAT YOU ARE BETTER THAN SOMEBODY ELSE IF YOU REALLY ARE BETTER?

## 63

**A:** Be careful not to fall into the trap of thinking of yourself as better. Who says you are better? Sometimes we believe that we are better than we are, and we become filled with pride. Be realistic about yourself, and humble, too. Remember that all of your abilities and talents are gifts from God. And all of us, even it we're good at something, need to depend on God. Remember that your relationship with God is most important.

There is nothing wrong with being glad that you did a good job at something—singing a solo, scoring points in a game, getting good grades, or being honest, for example. It's OK to feel good about yourself and to have confidence in what you do. You don't have to pretend that you aren't good or apologize for being good. But don't compare yourself to others or think of yourself as better than they are.

When someone pays you a compliment, say, "Thank you." Just remember that you may be a better basketball player, but that doesn't make you a better person.

---

**KEY VERSES:** *I am God's messenger. So I want to give each of you God's warning. Be honest when you think about yourself. Measure your value by how much faith God has given you. There are many parts to our bodies. It is the same with Christ's body. (Romans 12:3-4)*

**RELATED VERSES:** *Luke 18:9-14; James 4:6, 10*

**RELATED QUESTION:** *What does it mean to be humble?*

**NOTE TO PARENTS:** *Humility is a key part of developing healthy self-esteem. When your child feels down, offer affirmation. When your child feels inappropriate pride, remind him or her that all have sinned and fallen short of God's glory (Romans 3:23).*

# FAIR
## AND
# SQUARE
### (CHEATING)

# Q: IS IT OK TO SAY YOU TAGGED SOMEONE IN TAG WHEN YOU REALLY DIDN'T?

## 64

**A:** Saying that you tagged someone in a game when you didn't would be lying. God says that lying is wrong. Actually, cheating is always lying and always wrong, even in a fun game like tag. Rules make a game fun. If there were no rules, then no one would know how to play, and you wouldn't know who won or lost. Think of how silly it would be if, in tag, everyone tagged everyone else all the time. It wouldn't be any fun and certainly wouldn't be tag. In a good game, all the players follow the rules. Breaking the rules ruins the game.

This is more important than most people realize. The Bible says that if you are true and honest in "small matters," you will be true and honest in important ones. If you cheat in simple games, you may make cheating a habit in your life. Be honest in everything you do, even playing tag.

---

**KEY VERSE:** *Unless you are honest in small matters, you won't be in large ones. If you cheat even a little, you won't be honest with greater things. (Luke 16:10)*

**RELATED VERSES:** *Leviticus 19:35-36; 1 Samuel 8:1-3; Proverbs 11:1; 20:23; Matthew 25:14-30; 1 Timothy 3:8; Titus 1:7*

**RELATED QUESTION:** *Is it right if I cheat at something?*

**NOTE TO PARENTS:** *Encourage your children to take the smallest opportunities to be honest and fair. This will make it easier to be honest whenever a harder situation comes along, and it will make it easier for others to trust them in other matters.*

# Q: IS IT OK TO CHEAT AT A GAME WHEN THE GAME IS CALLED CHEAT AND THAT'S WHAT YOU'RE SUPPOSED TO DO?

## 65

**A:** It is too bad that this game is called Cheat, because it gives the idea that cheating is all right. Cheating is wrong because it's lying. When you are playing a game, no matter what it is called, you should play by the rules of the game. A game might call for players to make up stories about themselves, then people try to see which stories are true and which ones are false. That's not lying, because it's a game and everyone knows that the stories are made up. Even in a game like that, you should play by the rules. Games with funny rules can be fun. For example, you and your friends might want to make up new rules for a game of baseball in the snow. As long as everyone understands the rules and follows them, you can have a fun game. It will be different from regular baseball, but that's OK because everyone will be playing by the new rules.

You don't have to play every game. Some games are bad and can cause harm. Some games might make you do something that is wrong or something you know your parents would not approve of. In other words, play by the rules of every game unless it breaks God's rules!

---

**KEY VERSE:** *The Lord hates cheating and loves honesty. (Proverbs 11:1)*

**RELATED VERSES:** *Deuteronomy 25:16; Hosea 12:7*

**NOTE TO PARENTS:** *As a practical matter, make sure everyone understands the rules when you're playing a game. That way you can head off arguments about cheating.*

# Q: WHY IS IT WRONG TO LOOK AT SOMEONE'S SPELLING TEST AND WRITE THE WORDS DOWN?

## 66

**A:** When you look at a person's test or copy from another person's homework, you are not being honest. God commands us to be honest because he is truthful, and whenever our behavior is not like God's, we are wrong. When you look at someone else's answers on a test and then put the answers on your test, you are telling the teacher that you knew the right answer when you didn't. That is cheating—and lying. When you copy a friend's homework and turn it in, you are telling your teacher that you did the work by yourself when you didn't. That is cheating—and lying.

Remember that every time you lie or cheat you hurt youself in the long run. You are hurting yourself because you aren't learning what you need to learn, and someday you will regret it.

---

**KEY VERSE:** *Stop lying to each other. Tell the truth. We are part of each other. So when we lie to each other we are hurting ourselves. (Ephesians 4:25)*

**RELATED VERSES:** *Exodus 20:16; Leviticus 19:35-36; 1 Samuel 8:1-3; Proverbs 11:1; 20:23; Matthew 25:14-30; Luke 16:10; 1 Timothy 3:8; Titus 1:7*

**NOTE TO PARENTS:** *When a question like this arises, you can remind your child of the reasons for going to school and how cheating on a test undermines that purpose.*

# Q: WHAT'S SO BAD ABOUT CHEATING IN SPORTS?

## 67

**A:** Cheating in sports is bad because it deceives others and ruins the game. Sometimes on TV or even in school, it can seem as if winning a game is the most important thing in the world. We forget that it's only a game. We let winning become too important. But nothing is so important that we should cheat to get it, because God wants us to be honest, truthful, and fair in *all* that we do.

That's also why we should play clean. Some people think that playing dirty (hurting others in a game) is OK as long as it doesn't break any rules. But Christians should respect others as well as obey the rules.

Remember, the best reason to play sports is to improve our skills and physical condition and to learn about teamwork and how to win and *lose*. When we play any sport, we should do our best, play fair and clean, and enjoy the game. That's much more important than winning or losing.

---

**KEY VERSE:** *Unless you are honest in small matters, you won't be in large ones. If you cheat even a little, you won't be honest with greater things. (Luke 16:10)*

**RELATED VERSES:** *Leviticus 19:35-36; 1 Samuel 8:1-3; Proverbs 11:1; Matthew 25:14-30; Luke 16:10; Ephesians 4:25; 1 Timothy 3:8; Titus 1:7*

**NOTE TO PARENTS:** *Some parents put tremendous pressure on kids to succeed in sports. Don't lose perspective. If you put too much pressure on your children, you may unknowingly encourage them to cheat, thinking that winning matters more to you than playing well.*

# Q: IS IT CHEATING WHEN YOU LET THE OTHER TEAM WIN WHEN THEIR TEAM WASN'T PLAYING THAT WELL?

## 68

**A:** No. Cheating is when you break the rules in order to gain an advantage. You can play differently without breaking the rules. There are times when you might want to play easier to give another person or team a chance in a game. If you do, just be up-front about it.

But don't do it to make fun of them. If teams are very uneven and you know that one will slaughter the other, you may want to adjust the rules or change the teams to make it more even and thus more fun. Remember, what matters to God is that we treat each other with respect and love, not that we win.

**KEY VERSES:** *With the Holy Spirit in our lives there will be different kinds of fruit. They are love, joy, peace, patience, kindness, goodness, and faith. People with the Spirit are gentle and have self-control. (Galatians 5:22-23)*

**RELATED VERSE:** *Luke 6:31*

**NOTE TO PARENTS:** *Sometimes parents wonder whether they should go easy when playing games with their kids and let the children win. If children lose all the time, they will grow discouraged and quit. You could say, "I'll go easy on you to help you get the hang of it." And if it bothers your child that you let him or her win, promise to play harder next time—and do so. You'll both enjoy the challenge and have some fun. It's appropriate to give them some challenge—that's how they learn and grow.*

# Q: IF I CHEATED AND I WON, DO I HAVE TO TELL?

## 69

**A:** You shouldn't cheat in the first place. But if you did cheat, you should admit what you have done and make it right, whether you win or lose. In a game that's very important to you, you will feel the temptation to win at any cost. That's when you might think about cheating to gain an advantage. Just remember that winning is not the most important thing—doing what God wants is.

When you do something wrong and realize it, the best response is to confess. First, talk to God about what you have done. Then tell the other team or individual, and ask for forgiveness. You also may need to tell your parents.

Of course, telling afterward doesn't make the cheating right. In fact, you may have to pay back or give back what you took through cheating. Don't think you can cheat and then laugh about it later. God wants you to become an honest person.

---

**KEY VERSE:** *Tell each other when you do wrong. Pray for each other. Then you will be healed. The earnest prayer of a righteous man has great power and wonderful results. (James 5:16)*

**RELATED VERSES:** *Proverbs 11:1; 20:23; 1 John 1:9*

**NOTE TO PARENTS:** *This will be hard for kids. The typical response will be that they were just joking. But God doesn't want us to break his rules even temporarily. Help your child understand that if a person cheats and is caught, no one will believe that he or she was going to tell later, no matter what that person says about having innocent motives.*

# Q: WHEN YOU'RE PLAYING A GAME, IS IT OK TO FOOL THE OTHER PLAYERS?

## 70

A: In any game, it is all right to fool the other players if that's part of the game and doesn't break the rules. For example, in basketball a good player will fake a shot to fool the person guarding him or her. Or the player might pretend to go one direction and then go the other way. A good soccer player may fake a pass and then shoot instead. A good quarterback in football will pretend to hand off the ball to a halfback. All of these fakes are important parts of the sports—and within the bounds of the rules.

The important thing is to play fair and clean, within the rules. It would *not* be OK, for example, for a soccer player to fake a kick to the ball in order to kick another player. That would be cheating.

---

**KEY VERSE:** *You must do everything for God's glory, even your eating and drinking. (1 Corinthians 10:31)*

**RELATED VERSES:** *Proverbs 11:1; 20:23; Colossians 3:23-24*

**NOTE TO PARENTS:** *There is a difference between fooling others within the rules of the game and breaking the rules of the game in order to gain an unfair advantage. Be aware that some coaches will encourage players to fake an injury or be unnecessarily rough. The problem with that advice is that it bends or breaks the rules, not that it fools the other team.*

# Q: WHY DO PEOPLE CHEAT JUST TO WIN A STUPID GAME?

## 71

**A:** Some people cheat in sports or in a game because winning means too much to them. They have to win at everything. Maybe they like the feeling of power and control. Perhaps they like the attention that the winner receives. Maybe they really think they are better people because they win. They may even be desperate for respect and think people will only like them if they win. People who cheat don't understand that God loves them whether they win or lose.

God wants us to work hard at whatever we do and to do it well. If we are not very good at something and want to be able to do better, then we should practice more and try harder. If we cheat to win, we are taking a short cut, and we will have to keep on cheating in order to win.

Remember, when you play a game, play fair, play clean, and play by the rules. God wants you to do your best and to be honest. And whether you win or lose, you should be a good sport.

---

**KEY VERSES:** *Jealousy and selfishness are not God's kind of wisdom. Such things are earthly, unspiritual, and inspired by the devil. Wherever there is jealousy or ambition, there will be disorder and every kind of evil. (James 3:15-16)*

**RELATED VERSES:** *Proverbs 11:1; 20:23; 2 Corinthians 10:17; Philippians 2:3; James 1:15; 4:16*

**NOTE TO PARENTS:** *Affirm the character of kids who don't always brag about winning. You can illustrate this by talking about a favorite athlete who focuses on excelling rather than on bending the rules to win a game. Many people justify their cheating by saying, "I'm not the only one. Other people do it." Kids may do this, too. But that doesn't make it right.*

# Q: WHAT SHOULD I DO IF SOMEONE CHEATS ME?

## 72

**A:** If you are playing a sport like soccer and someone on the other team does something like kick the ball when it's out of bounds, let the referee deal with it. Don't call the player a cheater or argue with the referee. Be careful about saying that someone cheated you just because you lost a game. Maybe you lost fair and square.

If you are playing a game that has no referees, like a board game, and someone continues to cheat, you can tell the person that he or she is not playing fairly. Be sure to keep your cool and explain that cheating is wrong and that the game isn't fun when people cheat. If the person doesn't listen or continues to cheat, you don't have to keep playing.

If an adult cheats you out of money at a store, you should tell your parents and let them deal with it.

Sometimes, no one can help. Then it might be better just to accept the wrong and trust God to work it out OK.

---

**KEY VERSE:** *Don't get into needless fights. (Proverbs 3:30)*

**RELATED VERSES:** *Psalm 35:1-28; Luke 3:14; 1 Corinthians 6:7*

**NOTE TO PARENTS:** *If your children are complaining about someone who cheats, encourage them to pray for that person. Ask that God will show that person why cheating is wrong and why it doesn't help.*

# WHAT'S YOURS IS MINE
## (STEALING)

# Q: WHY IS IT WRONG TO STEAL THINGS?

## 73

**A:** God is honest and true. Taking what doesn't belong to you goes against God's nature. That is why stealing is wrong. God wants us to give to others, to help them, and to trust him to provide what we need.

Sometimes people steal because they want something (such as a bike, a tape player, or money) so badly that they will do anything to get it. Some people steal because they feel desperate. People who steal show that they don't trust God very much. God loves us and will never allow us to get into a situation where we have to steal something. He will provide what we need.

When you steal, you hurt God and yourself as much as you hurt the other person. You ignore and miss out on God's provision, get a bad reputation, and make other people feel like stealing from you. So you see, God really has our best interests in mind when he tells us not to steal.

---

**KEY VERSE:** *You must not steal. (Exodus 20:15)*

**RELATED VERSES:** *Matthew 6:25-34; Ephesians 4:28; Philippians 4:19; James 4:2*

# Q: IS IT OK TO STEAL SOMETHING BACK FROM SOMEONE WHO STOLE IT FROM YOU?

## 74

A: No. Stealing is always wrong. Be careful about accusing people of stealing. You may *think* someone stole something from you when he or she really didn't. If you are pretty sure that someone stole something from you, politely ask the person about the item. Perhaps you are wrong and the person only has something that *looks* like yours. If you go and take it back, you may end up taking something that really doesn't belong to you. Then *you* will be guilty of stealing!

If someone actually did take something from you, it's better to ask the person about it than to make an accusation of stealing, even if the item has your name on it. You could say something like: "I see you found my pen. Thank you for finding it." Always assume the best of the other person's motives.

If you catch someone stealing from you or you know that this person has been stealing from a lot of kids, first talk to the person about it. If that doesn't seem to help, then talk to an adult—a parent or teacher—about the problem.

**KEY VERSES:** *Never pay back evil for evil. Do things in a way that everyone can see you are honest. Don't argue with anyone. Be at peace with everyone as much as you can. (Romans 12:17-18)*

**RELATED VERSES:** *Exodus 20:15-16; Proverbs 3:30; Romans 2:21; 1 Corinthians 6:7; Ephesians 4:28*

**NOTE TO PARENTS:** *Handling a suspicion of stealing this way places the emphasis where it should be—on making friends instead of hurting people and making enemies.*

# Q: IS IT OK TO KEEP A TOY THAT BELONGS TO SOMEONE ELSE IF THEY DON'T ASK FOR IT BACK?

## 75

**A:** No. Stealing is taking something that doesn't belong to you. One type of stealing happens when a person borrows something from someone else but doesn't give it back. We know that stealing is wrong, all kinds of stealing, because God has told us not to steal. And if God has said it's wrong, then doing it will end up hurting us and others. Stealing is wrong and ends up hurting us even if no one finds out about it. Remember, God knows.

If a friend gives you something to keep, then that gift is yours. It would not be stealing to keep it—you don't have to give it back. But if someone loans you something or gives you something to use for a while, then you need to give it back when the time is up or when you are finished— even if the person doesn't ask for it or has forgotten about it. The same is true if you find something that belongs to someone else. You should give it to the person—that would be the honest thing to do.

God gives us the command not to steal. He does this to help us and to protect us from the penalties of stealing and the reputation of being a thief. Besides, isn't that the way you would want to be treated? Wouldn't you want your toy or book or ball returned, even if you had forgotten about it?

---

**KEY VERSE:** *Treat others as you want them to treat you. (Luke 6:31)*

**RELATED VERSES:** *Exodus 20:15; Ephesians 4:28*

**RELATED QUESTIONS:** *What if someone lends you something and you both forget about it? Is it stealing if you don't remember?*

# Q: WOULD IT BE WRONG IF YOUR FRIENDS TOLD YOU SOMETHING WAS FOR FREE, SO YOU TOOK IT, AND THEN YOU FOUND OUT LATER IT WASN'T REALLY FREE?

## 76

**A:** Wrongdoing is always wrong, even if we don't know it when we do it! Have you ever gone someplace you weren't supposed to go, said something you weren't supposed to say, or taken something you weren't supposed to take—without knowing you weren't supposed to? Everyone has at one time or another. Sometimes we don't find out until later that what we did was wrong. But when we find out, then what should we do? That's what really matters. We might have to ask for forgiveness or take something back. We certainly shouldn't do it again, now that we know better. For example, if friends said that something was free so you took it and then later you found out it wasn't free, you should take it back or pay for it. That would be the honest thing to do. Keeping it would be wrong.

Sometimes we just need to use common sense. For example, things in a store are hardly ever free. So if someone says they are, we should make sure by asking someone who works at the store. We shouldn't go along with *everything* our friends say. But we should go along with *everything* God says.

---

**KEY VERSE:** *You believe whatever anyone tells you. You believe even if he is preaching another Jesus than the one we preach. You welcome a different spirit than the Holy Spirit you received. If he shows you a different way to be saved, you swallow it all. (2 Corinthians 11:4)*

**RELATED VERSES:** *Luke 16:10; 1 Peter 1:13-16*

**RELATED QUESTION:** *What about when another kid tells you it's OK to do something, but you find out from an adult later on that it was wrong?*

# Q: IF IT'S WRONG TO STEAL, WHY DO THEY CALL IT "STEALING BASES" IN BASEBALL?

## 77

# A:

It's not really stealing; that's just the word they use to describe that kind of play. "Stealing bases" is part of the game of baseball. Baseball has other words that can be confusing, too: Batters are "walked" by the pitcher, some batters "sacrifice," the game is played on a "diamond," and the fourth base is called "home plate." Every game has its own special words and rules. To play any game the right way, it is important to know the rules and to understand what the special words mean. So "stealing" in baseball isn't the same as stealing in life. If someone really did *steal* second base, that person would pick the base up off the field and take it home. And that would be wrong!

---

**KEY VERSE:** *Young man, it's good to be young! Enjoy every minute of it! Do all you want to. Take in all you can. But know that you must account to God for all you do. (Ecclesiastes 11:9)*

**NOTE TO PARENTS:** *Be aware that kids sometimes don't understand the different meanings that a term can have. Encourage them to use words carefully because what we say has great power.*

# Q: IS IT WRONG TO COPY COMPUTER GAMES?

## 78

**A:** If a computer game is copyrighted, yes. What does *copyright* mean? It means that the person (or company) who created it is the only one with the right to copy it. People who write books, songs, magazine articles, and computer software often copyright their work so that other people can't sell or misuse it. The law says that anyone who *does* take or sell someone else's copyrighted work is guilty of stealing.

With stealing, usually we think of taking an object (money, a toy, a pencil, a hat, a ball, etc.) that belongs to someone else. But you can also steal information. When someone writes a song, the song belongs to that person. When someone writes a book, the book belongs to that person. Other people can have copies of the song or book if they *buy* them. Or someone could borrow another person's copy of the song or book. But it would be wrong just to *take* them—which is what happens when you make your own copies.

Remember, even if everybody does something wrong, it is still wrong because it still goes against God's nature.

---

**KEY VERSE:** *If anyone is stealing he must stop it. Let him begin by using his hands for honest work. Then he can give to others in need. (Ephesians 4:28)*

**RELATED VERSES:** *Exodus 20:15; Romans 13:1-5; 1 Peter 2:13-14*

**RELATED QUESTION:** *Is it right to record tapes?*

**NOTE TO PARENTS:** *Don't accept bootlegged copies of software or music for your kids, and don't make illegal copies for your own use. If you're unsure of what you can do with a particular program, check the license agreement that came with it.*

# Q: IS IT WRONG TO KEEP MONEY THAT YOU FIND ON THE STREET?

## 79

**A:** An honest person makes an honest effort to return things to their rightful owners, even when no one knows about it. With a wallet, the person could look for a name inside and contact the owner. With a large amount of money, the person could put up a sign or tell the police about it. Where the money is found is also important. Money found on a classroom floor was probably lost by someone in the class. Money found in a store was probably lost by someone who had just been in the store. In those cases, the person who found the money should tell the teacher or tell the store cashier. That would be the honest thing to do. The important thing is to do for the person who lost the money exactly what you would want them to do for you.

Sometimes it will be impossible to find the owner of the money. For example, you would probably never find the rightful owner of money found on the street or a dollar blowing across a field. But don't make excuses for keeping what doesn't belong to you—try to find the owner if you can.

---

**KEY VERSES:** *Jesus said, "'Love the Lord your God with all your heart, soul, and mind.' This is the first and greatest command. The second most important is similar: 'Love your neighbor as much as you love yourself.'" (Matthew 22:37-39)*

**RELATED VERSES:** *Deuteronomy 22:1-3; Luke 6:31-36*

**NOTE TO PARENTS:** *Kids have their own saying for this scenario: "Finders keepers, losers weepers." Tell your kids that God's greatest commandment gives us a different standard—one that respects people and looks out for their best interests.*

# Q: IS IT STEALING IF A POOR PERSON TAKES FOOD?

## 80

**A:** Yes. No matter what a person steals or why, it is still stealing.

The Bible says a lot about poor people. God's people, the nation of Israel, were supposed to help the poor. And hungry people were allowed to gather leftover grain from the fields (called gleaning). But the poor were never told that they were allowed to steal food.

There are many poor and hungry people in the world. We should do whatever we can to help them (sending food, donating money to relief organizations) so they won't be tempted to steal food.

---

**KEY VERSES:** *O God, I beg two favors from you before I die. First, help me never to tell a lie. Second, give me neither poverty nor riches! Give me just enough to satisfy my needs! For if I grow rich, I may become content without God. And if I am too poor, I may steal. That way I might insult God's holy name. (Proverbs 30:7-9)*

**RELATED VERSES:** *Exodus 20:15; Leviticus 19:10; 23:22; Deuteronomy 24:19-21; Proverbs 19:17; Matthew 6:19-21, 25-34; Acts 2:42-45; James 2:14-16*

**NOTE TO PARENTS:** *When your child asks a question like this, it's a great opportunity for you as a family to begin to support a relief agency or sponsor a child or family. It is also a good opportunity to pray together that God will meet your own family's daily needs and thank him for doing so.*

# Q: IS IT STEALING TO BORROW SOMEONE ELSE'S STUFF WITHOUT ASKING?

## 81

**A:** It sure can be. Borrowing anything from anybody without asking doesn't show much respect for the owner. What if the owner needed it right away or had promised it to someone else? It always is best to ask permission to borrow something, even if it belongs to a good friend and you have used it before.

If the person has told you something like, "Use it anytime you want," and he or she isn't around to ask, that's different. You can go ahead and borrow it and leave a note. You want the person to know that it wasn't stolen and that *you* borrowed it. Asking permission and leaving notes show respect for your friend. Don't ever steal something and then make the excuse that you were "just borrowing it." Stealing is wrong, and so is lying. Be an honest person who respects others and their property.

---

**KEY VERSE:** *Treat others as you want them to treat you. (Luke 6:31)*

**RELATED VERSES:** *Exodus 20:15; Matthew 22:34-40; Ephesians 4:28*

**NOTE TO PARENTS:** *Siblings often fight over toys when they're young and over each other's clothes when they're older. This is an opportunity to teach children how to share and be generous. Kids don't learn this naturally; they need you to teach them.*

# Q: WHAT IF SOMEONE IS SHOP-LIFTING AND IT IS YOUR FRIEND—WHAT DO YOU DO?

STEEL
BALL BEARINGS

## 82

# A:

If you know that your friend is going to steal something or is trying to do so, you should point out that stealing is wrong and he or she shouldn't do it. If your friend doesn't want to listen to you, you should walk away, leave the store or wherever you are, and go home right away. Being with a person who is breaking the law can get you into trouble, too, because it is a crime not to report a crime. Tell your parents as soon as you get home.

---

**KEY VERSES:** *Now suppose, brothers, someone slips away from God. Such a person no longer trusts in the Lord. But then someone helps him understand the Truth again. The person who brings him back to God will have saved a soul from death. He will bring about the forgiveness of his many sins. (James 5:19-20)*

**RELATED VERSES:** *Exodus 20:15; Proverbs 1:10-14; 13:20; Romans 13:1-5; 2 Thessalonians 3:14-15; Hebrews 10:24*

**RELATED QUESTION:** *If I see my friend steal, what do I do?*

**NOTE TO PARENTS:** *Help your child know how to pick friends and when it's time to stop being friends with someone. We want our kids to be positive influences, but there comes a time when they need to dissociate themselves from troublemakers.*

**Q:** WHAT IF YOU FIND SOME-THING THAT DOESN'T BELONG TO YOU AND YOU CAN'T FIND WHO IT BELONGS TO—IS THAT STEALING?

## 83

**A:** Finding something that doesn't belong to you isn't stealing, but you should try to find the owner if you can. How hard you try should match the value of what you find. A penny or nickel is worth very little; you don't need to put an ad in the paper to find the person who lost it. But an album of wedding pictures, a box of jewelry, or a wallet is worth a great deal. You should make a far greater effort to find the owner of such valuable items. Often your mom or dad will know exactly how to look for this person. If you find something at school, you can take it to the lost and found. Never use the statement "I just found it and can't see anybody around" as an excuse to call something yours.

---

**KEY VERSES:** *You might see someone's ox or sheep wandering away. If you do, don't pretend you didn't see it. Take it back to its owner. You might not know who the owner is. If so, take it to your farm and keep it there. When the owner comes looking for it, then give it to him. The same applies to donkeys, clothing, or anything else you find. Keep it for its owner. (Deuteronomy 22:1-3)*

**RELATED VERSE:** *Philippians 2:4*

**RELATED QUESTIONS:** *Is it wrong to keep a $20 bill that you found on the ground even when someone asked you if you saw it? If you find a coin in a candy machine and you use it in the machine to buy candy, is that stealing?*

**NOTE TO PARENTS:** *Give examples of when you did this or when it was done to you and how you felt. You might also mention to your children that people will notice whenever they make an attempt to return something.*

# LAST
## BUT
# NOT
# LEAST

# Q: IS IT ALL RIGHT TO THROW ROCKS AT SOMEONE WHO THREW ROCKS AT YOU?

DAVID & GOLIATH PLAY KIT

## 84

**A:** It is not right to do something bad to someone just because that person did something bad to us. The Bible calls that "returning evil for evil," and Jesus says it is wrong. The Bible also tells us that we shouldn't try to get back at people who hurt us. We do not have the right to punish people for the things they do wrong. Instead we should talk about the situation with God and leave it with him. It's all right to protect ourselves, but it's not OK to get even.

This may seem unfair. But actually, only God knows how to judge fairly—we don't. By refusing to return evil for evil, we let God take care of making things right. And God is perfect in all his judgments.

Just because someone else is sinning doesn't give us the excuse to sin. We should always try to obey God and do what is right. God's way is always best. Getting back at others usually doesn't solve the problem; it just makes things worse.

---

**KEY VERSES:** *The law of Moses says, "A man might gouge out another man's eye. If this happens, he must pay with his own eye. If a tooth gets knocked out, knock out the tooth of the one who did it." But I say don't stand against violence! If you are slapped on one cheek, turn the other one, too. (Matthew 5:38-39)*

**RELATED VERSES:** *Proverbs 20:22; Luke 6:27-36; Acts 7:60; Romans 12:17-21*

**RELATED QUESTIONS:** *Is it wrong to yell at my parents when they tell me no? Is it wrong to be angry at my brother after he broke something of mine? Should you be mean to someone who was really mean to your sister?*

LAST BUT NOT LEAST

# Q: IS IT ALL RIGHT TO SAY BAD THINGS IF THERE IS NO ONE THERE TO HEAR YOU?

## 85

**A:** If something is wrong, then it is wrong even if no one else ever finds out about it. So swearing, lying, and saying bad things about others are wrong, even if our parents, friends, neighbors, and everyone else can't hear. God knows what's going on; he sees and hears everything.

That's why a true test of your character comes whenever you think no one else is watching or listening. If you really believe that swearing is wrong, you won't do it, period. You won't look for opportunities to do it when no one is around to catch you. Work hard at speaking and *thinking* what is good and right, even when no one else is around, because that's what really matters. Even what you think counts; God knows our every thought.

And if anyone ever does find out what you said in private, they will know that you can be trusted. Live every moment as a service to God.

---

**KEY VERSE:** *Don't use bad language. Say only what is good and helpful to those you are talking to. That will give them a blessing. (Ephesians 4:29)*

**RELATED VERSES:** *Proverbs 5:21; 20:11; Ecclesiastes 12:14; Philippians 4:8*

**RELATED QUESTION:** *Is it wrong to swear under your breath?*

**NOTE TO PARENTS:** *Kids often think that if a deed doesn't hurt anybody, it's OK. But wrong actions always hurt someone in some way in the long run. The damage may be indirect or take time to become obvious, such as when chronic lying destroys trust in a family. But in the end, everything we do has an effect on others.*

# Q: CAN I DO WHATEVER I WANT WHEN I'M OLDER?

## 86

**A:** Some kids think that when they grow up they will be able to do anything they want. And it may appear that some adults live that way. But that's not true. All our lives we will have rules and laws to obey. When God gave the Ten Commandments, he gave them to all people, of all ages, for all time. No one outgrows the need to follow God's ways. We should always obey God.

That's one of the reasons God tells us to obey our parents. Doing what they say helps us learn to obey those in authority over us later in life. It also helps us want to do what's right.

**KEY VERSE:** *Don't let anyone think little of you because you are young. Be their example. Let them follow the way you teach and live. Be a pattern for them in your love, your faith, and your clean thoughts. (1 Timothy 4:12)*

**RELATED VERSES:** *John 14:6; 1 Corinthians 6:12; 1 Peter 5:1-4*

**RELATED QUESTION:** *Why do grown-ups yell at each other?*

**NOTE TO PARENTS:** *The question behind the question here may be about double standards. If parents do something they forbid kids to do, it will appear to the children that adults can do whatever they want. Don't use your age to justify wrong behavior.*

# Q: IS THINKING SOMETHING BAD THE SAME AS DOING IT OR SAYING IT?

## 87

**A:** No. Hating someone and wishing that person were dead are both terrible, but hating only affects the person who is thinking the bad thoughts. He or she would make the situation much worse by actually killing the other person. The same is true with stealing, lying, and other bad thoughts. As wrong as it is to think bad thoughts, it's even worse to do them or say them.

But our thoughts *are* important, because we often end up doing what we keep thinking about. Suppose your mother told you not to eat any cookies before dinner. But you see the cookies on the counter and keep thinking about how good they would taste, especially with a glass of cold milk. If you keep thinking about this, the desire to eat those cookies will probably grow and grow until eventually you might disobey your mom and take some.

God knows what we are thinking, and he wants us to fill our minds with good thoughts, not bad.

---

**KEY VERSE:** *O Jerusalem, make your hearts clean while there is still time. You can still be saved by throwing out your evil thoughts. (Jeremiah 4:14)*

**RELATED VERSES:** *1 Chronicles 28:9; Philippians 4:8; James 1:14-15*

**RELATED QUESTION:** *Is it wrong to think bad thoughts?*

**NOTE TO PARENTS:** *At some point most children become concerned about being punished by God for their bad thoughts. Let your child know that it's not wrong to have a bad thought, but it is wrong to keep on thinking about it instead of thinking about something else. Make sure your child understands why it's wrong to dwell on bad thoughts: Our thoughts grow into desires and actions.*

# Q: WHY IS IT WRONG TO DO SOMETHING IF ALL THE OTHER KIDS DO IT?

PRIVATE PROPERTY
<u>NO</u>
SKATE BOARDING

## 88

**A:** If something is wrong, it's wrong, no matter how many people do it. Suppose a group of your friends started throwing stones through windows in the neighborhood. Would it be OK just because everyone did it? Of course not! It would be wrong whether *one* person or *everyone in school* did it. You can be sure that the police and the homeowners would say it was wrong!

If a lot of kids swear, cheat, lie, do drugs, drink, smoke, disobey their parents, shoplift, or do something else that is wrong, don't think that you have to do it, too. You should do what is right, even if you are the only one. That's what God wants.

If the group you hang around with does things that are wrong and pressures you to join them, find another group. Get away from kids who are always tempting you to do wrong.

---

**KEY VERSES:** *I am speaking for the Lord. Don't live like the unsaved do anymore. They are blinded and confused. Their closed hearts are full of darkness. They are far away from the life of God. Why? Because they have shut their minds against him. They can't understand his ways. They don't care anymore about right and wrong. They have given themselves over to doing wrong things. They stop at nothing. They are driven by their evil minds and reckless lusts. (Ephesians 4:17-19)*

**RELATED VERSES:** *Judges 2:11-15; Romans 12:1-2; Colossians 2:8*

**NOTE TO PARENTS:** *Peer pressure on kids can be quite strong. As your child grows older, you can help combat peer pressure by spending time together one-on-one and together as a family.*

# Q: SHOULD I TELL ON OTHER KIDS?

## 89

**A:** If a law will be broken or someone will be hurt, yes. God puts adults in positions of authority to protect you and others against wrongdoing. If those adults don't know about a problem, they can't provide that protection. Tell a parent, teacher, coach, counselor, police officer, or another concerned adult if someone is stealing, doing drugs, selling drugs, drinking, planning to break the law, talking about committing suicide, or talking about hurting someone. There's nothing wrong with telling on other kids at times like that.

But there *is* something wrong with "telling on" kids you don't like just to get them in trouble. Remember, you aren't a parent, teacher, principal, or police officer. Also, if you tell on someone and that person gets into trouble, don't brag and make a big deal about what you did. God's purpose for us is to serve him and help others—that's the reason for telling in the first place—so bragging is out of place.

**KEY VERSE:** *Take no part in the worthless pleasures of evil and darkness. Instead, rebuke them and bring them out into the light. (Ephesians 5:11)*

**RELATED VERSES:** *Luke 17:3; Romans 13:1-5; 1 Peter 2:13-14*

**NOTE TO PARENTS:** *The issue of tattling on other kids is very real—kids hate tattlers so much that some parents encourage their kids not to tell on anybody at any time, fearing that they will lose friends. But it's important for kids to report wrongdoing—it's a basic part of being a responsible friend and citizen. Teach your child to enforce the rules out of a desire to help others respond properly to God, rather than appearing morally superior.*

# Q: WHY DO PEOPLE LITTER?

## 90

**A:** Some people litter because it's a habit. Others just don't really care. No matter why people litter, it is against the law and hurts the environment. Littering shows a lack of respect for others and their property, and it makes everything look ugly. Christians should respect other people, other people's property, God's creation, and the law. So we should not litter.

---

**KEY VERSE:** *Then God said, "Let us make a man—someone like ourselves. He will be the master of all life upon the earth and in the skies and in the seas." (Genesis 1:26)*

**RELATED VERSE:** *Luke 6:31*

**RELATED QUESTION:** *Does God let pollution up into heaven?*

**NOTE TO PARENTS:** *Kids often have the mentality that "I didn't make the mess so I don't have to clean it up." We need to teach our kids to take responsibility for the environment. If you see litter, pick it up. Keep some kind of bag for trash in your car. Set an example for your child in this area.*

# Q: WHY IS IT NOT GOOD TO TALK TO STRANGERS?

## 91

**A:** Sadly, there are a lot of bad people in the world. Some of these people want to do bad things to children. That's why children are told not to talk to strangers. God does not have a rule against it in the Bible, so it's not wrong in that way. But God has said to obey your parents, so it would be wrong to disobey your mom or dad if they told you not to talk to adults you don't know. Even if your parents haven't said anything, it would be *wise* to stay away from strangers. Of course, some "strangers" are good people, and some may even need help. But still it is a good rule to stay away from adults you don't know.

So it's not *wrong* to talk to a stranger, it just could be dangerous. That's why your parents tell you not to do it. They don't want you to put yourself in a place where a stranger who is a bad person could hurt you. If a stranger asks you for help or you see someone in trouble, get your mom or dad or another adult that you know. Don't try to help by yourself.

---

**KEY VERSE:** *In the last days there will come scoffers. They will do every wrong they can think of. And they will laugh at the truth. (2 Peter 3:3)*

**RELATED VERSES:** *Proverbs 14:15; Romans 16:17-18; Ephesians 6:1-3*

**NOTE TO PARENTS:** *One way to help your child learn how to talk to strangers is to role-play. This can give the child the opportunity to practice what to say and do before a scary situation arises. Also, explain that in the proper context and situations God requires us to be kind to new people we meet.*

# Q: IS IT OK TO BEG FOR THINGS FROM YOUR PARENTS?

## 92

**A:** It is OK to *ask* your parents for things, but not to beg. For example, you could ask for a special treat, Christmas presents, or permission to go to a friend's house or stay up late. You should ask politely and explain your reasons. But if they say no, you should accept their answer with a good attitude. Don't beg. That is, don't ask over and over and over to try to get them to give you what they really don't want to give you. Don't try to wear them down.

The key is simply to respect your parents. They gave their answer because they thought it was best for you. If you wear them down, you may get what you want and then regret it later. God gave you parents to protect you and provide for you. If you talk them into going against their first answer, you step outside that protection. Respect and obey your mom and dad.

---

**KEY VERSE:** *When you do ask you don't get it because your whole aim is wrong. You want only what will make you happy. (James 4:3)*

**RELATED VERSES:** *Exodus 20:12; Ephesians 6:1-3; Colossians 3:20*

**NOTE TO PARENTS:** *Don't let a child wear you down with nagging. (More to the point, don't allow the child to nag!) And when your child does push or beg, don't give in unless you have a good reason. Also, affirm your children every time they make a polite request, respond the right way to your answers, and have a positive attitude. Finally, always think about your answer before giving it. If the answer could be or should be yes, but you say no for convenience, you'll probably change your mind when your child nags you. And that will encourage nagging with every no!*

LAST BUT NOT LEAST

## 93

**A:** No, because the Bible says that we should have self-control. That means God wants us to control our emotions, not let them control us. Emotions are good, and it is good to understand what we are feeling. In other words, if we are angry, we shouldn't pretend we aren't. But we should also think about why we are angry, talk to God and others about it, and work at changing what caused the anger. And we have to be careful about how we express our anger—yelling, screaming, calling names, hitting, and slamming doors can hurt other people, making the situation worse. If you are polite, people will be more likely to listen and pay attention to your concerns.

---

**KEY VERSE:** *It is better to be slow-tempered than famous. It is better to have self-control than to control an army. (Proverbs 16:32)*

**RELATED VERSES:** *Galatians 5:19-23; Ephesians 4:26; Colossians 3:8; James 1:19-20*

**RELATED QUESTIONS:** *Is it wrong to get angry at a teacher if she treats you unfairly? Is it wrong to get angry?*

**NOTE TO PARENTS:** *Handling anger well takes practice. You can help your child learn this valuable skill in several ways: (1) If a question about anger comes up, talk together about alternatives to slamming doors, shouting, or stomping around. Ask, "What else could you do to let me know you're upset?" (2) The next time your child gets angry enough to slam a door, encourage him or her to tell you about it ("I'm angry because . . .") and be sure to listen patiently. (3) Whenever you are angry, set an example that your child can see and copy.*

# Q: WHY DO I HAVE TO DO CHORES?

## 94

**A:** Three reasons: (1) Good families work together. (2) Good family members want to help the family. (3) Doing chores is a way of taking responsibility, which is a part of growing up.

When children are very young, the parents do most of the work around the house. As children get older, they begin to help out as they are able. Many families assign special jobs, or "chores," to each person in the family. This way, everyone in the family can help make sure that everything in the house runs smoothly and the work gets done. Chores can include setting the table, cleaning and dusting, cutting the grass, shoveling the snow, washing clothes, washing windows, cooking meals, and even fixing the car—depending on the age and ability of the person.

When your parents give you chores to do, think of it as a compliment and an opportunity. They know you can handle the job. And you can be a helpful member of the family.

Remember, your parents aren't just trying to get you to do their work for them. They are preparing you for life. If you can learn now to be diligent and helpful, it will save you a lot of trouble when you grow up.

---

**KEY VERSE:** *Some won't even care for their own relatives. They won't even take care of those living in their own family. But they have no right to say they are Christians. Such people are worse than the heathen. (1 Timothy 5:8)*

**RELATED VERSES:** *Exodus 20:12; 2 Thessalonians 3:10; 1 Timothy 4:12*

**RELATED QUESTION:** *Is it a sin not to clean your room when your mom and dad have asked you to?*

# Q: WHY DO I HAVE TO BRUSH MY TEETH?

## 95

**A:** If your parents tell you to brush your teeth, then you should do it. God wants children to obey their parents. But there's another reason for brushing your teeth. You see, each person is a very special creation of our loving God. He has given us bodies to live in and to use for serving him. It is our job to take care of our bodies and to use them well. This means eating the right food, getting enough sleep, watching our weight, exercising, dressing warmly in cold weather, and not hurting ourselves with drugs, alcohol, and tobacco. It also means brushing our teeth and keeping ourselves clean.

It wouldn't be a sin if an adult didn't brush his teeth one day. It *would* be a sin, however, if he didn't take care of his teeth and let them get decayed. It's not a sin to eat candy. But it would be sinful if a person only ate candy and destroyed her health. God wants us to take care of our bodies.

---

**KEY VERSE:** *Don't you know that your body is the home of the Holy Spirit? The Holy Spirit lives within you! Your own body does not belong to you. (1 Corinthians 6:19)*

**RELATED VERSE:** *Song of Solomon 4:2*

**RELATED QUESTIONS:** *Why do I have to take a bath? Why do I have to go to bed early every night? Why should I have manners? Why do I have to wash my hands every time I eat?*

**NOTE TO PARENTS:** *Be careful not to make conflicts over hygiene too big an issue. In fact, a wise parent will make it enjoyable. For example, you can tape a fun note to the toothbrush every night or offer to play a game as a family when everyone finishes brushing.*

# Q: IS IT OK TO TELL PEOPLE TO SHUT UP IF THEY ARE BEING JERKS?

## 96

**A:** When someone does something annoying or wrong, we don't have to like it. But we shouldn't do something bad to them in return. God wants us to be loving and kind to others. So the rule is to be respectful, not bossy or rude. If the person will listen to your opinion, say something, but say it kindly. Sometimes it's *good* to tell friends that they're not being nice or that they are being mean. You don't have to like someone else's cruelty, but you don't have to respond just like they do, either.

God knows that it's best for us when we do things his way. Responding to cruelty with kindness makes friends of people. But when we respond to cruelty with cruelty, we just feed the conflict and make more conflict. So the best way to make someone stop annoying you is to be nice to the person, not mean.

**KEY VERSE:** *A gentle answer turns away anger. But harsh words cause fights. (Proverbs 15:1)*

**RELATED VERSES:** *Proverbs 4:24; 12:16; Romans 12:17; 15:2; James 2:8; 1 Peter 2:17*

**RELATED QUESTION:** *Is it wrong to call other people names?*

**NOTE TO PARENTS:** *Don't let kids say cruel and unkind things to each other or to you. It's simply a matter of respecting others not to say shut up or other disrespectful words to people. Instead, show them how to discuss the concerns they have with each other without attacking. Help them solve problems instead of fighting over them.*

# Q: WHY DO PEOPLE SAY THINGS THAT AREN'T TRUE ABOUT THE STUFF THEY SELL ON COMMERCIALS?

## 97

**A:** Companies make commercials to try to get people to buy their products. Some companies don't care what they say, even if it's not true. They just want to get people to buy their stuff. All commercials try to make the product look good. So they may not lie, but they may give an impression that isn't true. For example, a TV ad may show a group of kids having great fun playing a game. We really don't know whether the game is fun—the kids on TV are actors who were paid to look as if they were having fun. We are led to believe that it would make us happy to play the game.

When you see or hear an advertisement, look and listen carefully. Also, don't get into the habit of wanting everything that looks good on TV. You probably don't need it, and it may not be as good as it looks anyway.

---

**KEY VERSE:** *Don't let others spoil your faith and joy with their philosophies. They give wrong and shallow answers built on men's thoughts and ideas. The things they teach are not built on what Christ has said. (Colossians 2:8)*

**RELATED VERSES:** *Luke 12:15; 2 Timothy 3:1-9; 1 John 2:15-17*

**NOTE TO PARENTS:** *Some kids don't know that commercials can create false impressions, because they don't have the benefit of experience that you have. You can turn commercials into an educational experience by pointing out how they may be misleading the audience. Perhaps you have a story of how an ad had this effect on you.*

# Q: WHY SHOULDN'T WE TAKE DRUGS?

## 98

# A:

Prescription drugs (medicine) are OK to take. In fact, doctors give those to us to help make us well when we're sick. We must carefully obey the doctor's instructions about when to take them and how much to take so the drugs can help us. Taking drugs in the wrong way can be very bad for us. That's why there are laws about them.

Drugs that can hurt us are against the law. Some people use these drugs because it makes them feel good for a little while. But often they get hooked, and the drugs take over their lives. They affect people's brains so that they can't think right, and they can even kill people.

We shouldn't let anything we put into our bodies control us, whether it's food, drink, drugs, alcohol, or any other chemical. Only God should be in control of our lives. And God wants us to take care of our bodies—bad drugs destroy our bodies. Stay far away from all illegal drugs.

---

**KEY VERSE:** *Don't drink too much wine. Many evils lie along that path. Be filled instead with the Holy Spirit and be controlled by him. (Ephesians 5:18)*

**RELATED VERSE:** *1 Corinthians 6:19*

**RELATED QUESTIONS:** *Why is it wrong to drink? Why is it wrong to smoke? Is it wrong to smoke even one cigarette? Why do people take drugs? Why do we have drugs?*

# Q: WHY DO SOME WHITE AND BLACK PEOPLE HATE EACH OTHER?

## 99

**A:** Hate is another problem caused by sin in the world. People get angry and hate others for many reasons. They may be upset over something a person said or did—they may feel insulted or hurt. They may be bitter about what a person's relatives did in the past. But hate is wrong. God tells us to love, not hate. If someone hurts us, we should forgive that person and try to fix the relationship.

Some people hate others for very silly reasons. They may not like another person's religion, nationality, neighborhood, school, or skin color. For a long time, many white people have hated black people just because they are black. And many black people have hated white people just because they are white. And people have been mean and cruel to other kinds of people, too, such as Hispanics, and Japanese or Irish people.

That is not God's way. God's way is for all kinds of people to live together, to work together, and to worship together. We should show love and respect to all people, no matter how different they are from us.

---

**KEY VERSE:** *We are no longer Jews or Gentiles. We are no longer slaves or free men. We are not even men or women. We are all the same, we are Christians. We are one in Christ Jesus. (Galatians 3:28)*

**RELATED VERSES:** *Colossians 3:11-14; James 2:14-17; 1 John 4:20-21; Revelation 7:9; 20:11-15*

**NOTE TO PARENTS:** *Watch your own words and actions. Go out of your way to have positive relationships with people who differ from you. Show your child by word and example how to treat all people with equal respect.*

# Q: IF I SEE SOMEONE WHO IS POOR, DO I HAVE TO GIVE THAT PERSON MONEY?

## 100

A: There are a lot of poor people in the world. Many people beg for money so that they can buy food. It makes us sad to see people beg, and we wish we could help everybody. Sometimes we walk by many people who are asking for money. Obviously we can't give money to every poor person. If we did that, we would run out of money very soon and be poor ourselves. But we can and should help *some* poor people. We can help people in the neighborhood by working around their homes and giving them food. We can give money to our churches and Christian organizations to help poor people in our community and around the world. We can give our time at a local mission. God wants us to be loving and kind to people. He wants us to show his love to widows, prisoners, the poor, and the hungry. When we help poor people, we are acting like Jesus.

---

**KEY VERSE:** *There will always be some among you who are poor. That is why this command is needed. You must lend to them as they have need. (Deuteronomy 15:11)*

**RELATED VERSES:** *Exodus 23:10-11; Leviticus 25:35; Amos 8:4-6; Matthew 25:34-40; Luke 4:18; James 2:2-6*

**RELATED QUESTIONS:** *Is it OK to pray for toys and things? Why should I give money to God?*

**NOTE TO PARENTS:** *There are small ways you can foster a sharing attitude at home. Also, you can find ways to give as a family. You can donate clothes, furniture, time, or other resources to ministries that serve the poor. And when you have things that are useful and in good condition that you no longer need, don't sell the good stuff and give away junk; that's convenience, not compassion.*

## 101

**A:** A rumor (or gossip) is a story about someone or something that everybody talks about without really knowing whether it's true or not. Sometimes rumors are totally false, but they are spread because somebody got the wrong information. Sometimes rumors are deliberate lies, spread to hurt someone. Sometimes rumors are partially true, but they don't tell the whole story. Even if a story started out to be true, after a few people tell it, it usually gets changed and is only partly true. Rumors almost always do much more harm than good.

If you hear a bad story about someone, don't just pass it on. First, try to find out whether it is true or not. If you find out that the story is true, you have two good choices: (1) You can drop it and forget the whole thing, or (2) you can talk to the person that the story is about and try to help. God wants us to be loving and kind to others. Passing along gossip, spreading rumors, is not loving or kind.

---

**KEY VERSE:** *An evil person plants trouble. Gossip pulls the best of friends apart. (Proverbs 16:28)*

**RELATED VERSES:** *Proverbs 20:19; 2 Corinthians 12:20*

**RELATED QUESTION:** *Why is it wrong to gossip?*

**NOTE TO PARENTS:** *Remember that your child learns from the way you talk about others. Make an effort not to confuse facts with guesses in your discussions about other people.*

# Q: IS IT OK TO DRIVE MY DAD'S CAR FOR FOUR SECONDS?

## 102

**A:** If you drive a car on a public street and don't have a driver's license, you are breaking the law. If you drive a car on private property (for example, a driveway) and don't have a driver's license, you are being very foolish. This is true no matter how long you drive the car—four seconds or four hours. A car is a huge machine with a lot of power. It can be very dangerous to you and to others. That's why people have to be trained to drive and why they have to pass a driving test to get a license.

---

**KEY VERSE:** *Be very sure to follow all the laws written in the book of Moses. Do not disobey them the least little bit. (Joshua 23:6)*

**RELATED VERSE:** *James 2:10*

**NOTE TO PARENTS:** *This kind of question may arise out of a child's judgment that it's OK to obey only the letter of the law. Also, some kids will try to see whether a rule can be broken under any circumstances at all, so that they can then expand the rule breaking into further territory. If it's OK to drive the car for four seconds, isn't it OK to drive it for eight seconds?*

# Q: WHAT IF I TOLD A LIE AND DIDN'T KNOW IT WAS A LIE— IS IT STILL A LIE?

# A:

To pass on information that you *think* is true but really isn't, is *not* lying. But what you say can be wrong and can hurt somebody. That's why it is so important to check out the facts to see if something is true, especially if the information sounds fishy or you're not very sure. Suppose you heard from a friend that the school concert would begin at 8:00, but it really is going to begin at 7:30. It would be good to find out for sure before telling your parents about the concert. Just think how they would feel if they showed up half an hour late.

Beware of talking too much. Being slow to speak will help you avoid getting into trouble with your words. It's to your own benefit for people to know that they can rely on what you say. And if you are afraid that you lied without knowing it, tell God about it. He will forgive you.

**KEY VERSE:** *Dear brothers, remember this! It is best to listen much, speak little, and not become angry. (James 1:19)*

**RELATED VERSES:** *Proverbs 14:3; 17:28; 18:21; 29:20; Ecclesiastes 5:2; Colossians 4:6; Hebrews 10:24*

**NOTE TO PARENTS:** *Help your children learn to say "I don't know" or "I'm not sure" if they don't have all the facts. For example, "I'm not sure, but I think it starts at 8:00" is better than "It starts at 8:00." Tell your children that it's OK not to be certain. Then they will be less likely to pass on incorrect information to you or others.*

# For more answers to tough questions be sure to check out the rest of the series . . .

101 QUESTIONS CHILDREN ASK ABOUT GOD    0-8423-5102-7

102 QUESTIONS CHILDREN ASK ABOUT THE BIBLE    08423-4570-1